D0122408

CORPORATE LUNACY

How to win (or at least survive) the corporate game

CORPORATE
LUNACY

How to win (or at least survive) the corporate game

REALITY
PRESS

RA McMillan

Illustrated By Douglas Goldsmith

Library of Congress Catalog Card Number: 00-190808
ISBN: 0-9678568-0-9

For Chris, a beacon of sanity, and my refuge from the storm, and to the memory of Joe Snyder, my mentor, and friend.

Corporate Lunacy

CONTENTS

ACKNOWLEDGEMENTS

Writing this book required the assistance and support of many friends, business associates and family members over a number of years. Of course, the greatest appreciation must go to Chris, my wife and best friend, for her encouragement. Dale Parker, you're an inspiration. Tom Williams, you've been a terrific help. David Rogers and Dave Hatch, you've always provided wise counsel. Tom, Dick, Pat and Ray, thanks. I owe special gratitude to A.J. Ashe, a valued mentor and friend. A.J., you hired me and introduced me to the wonderful, wacky world of corporate America.

The situations described in this book are absolutely factual (Okay, maybe I've exaggerated a bit). So, recognition must go to those incomprehensible and infuriating corporate dwellers that provided the stimulus for much of the book. If you think you spot yourself here, you're welcome!

Much of the best material came from my own foibles and weaknesses as a manager. I am grateful that Tom, Keith, Dave, Scott and Sandi refrained from reminding me continually of these shortcomings.

A special debt is owed to Bill Fryer, my editor, who took a poorly organized mishmash and helped me create a book. Julie Kopmeyer did a superb job of editing grammar and punctuation and she even extracted a bit of venom. Doug Goldsmith created the marvelous illustrations, capturing the spirit of the manuscript. Many thanks must go to the staff of Ansley & Associates for bringing it all together. Janet Zambelli, D Ben Woods, Heather Usner, Brian Roach and Elizabeth Ricchiuti provided essential help in graphic design, copy review and organization. You hired a great group, Jim and Joan.

There are countless other people I should thank but I can't remember their names. That's probably merciful because they may not want to be associated with this book. It would also be appropriate to thank my psychologist, but the therapeutic value of writing this book allowed me to avoid one.

Joe Snyder, I dedicate this book to your memory. You cured my naivete, helping me to accept the world as it is, not as I wish it to be.

Corporate Lunacy

INTRODUCTION

"Now, here, you see, it takes all the running you can do, to keep in the same place. If you want to get somewhere else, you must run at least twice as fast as that!"
Lewis Carroll (1832-98)

The modern corporation can be an exciting place. Unlike those boring old-style businesses in which hard work and a sense of responsibility carried you up the ladder of success, the new corporate world is so large, so intellectually incoherent, so fixated on appearances, so focused on right now, that old rules do not apply.

Do you need to work hard? Probably not, although the appearance of doing so helps. Do you need to be responsible? Responsible to whom and for what? Do you need to be loyal, form firm alliances and lifelong business friendships? Seriously, now. What is a "business friendship?"

This is the modern corporation, remember. If you want to get rid of some of the venom accumulated during your disastrous high school social career, opportunity knocks. The subtle undercut, the verbal sideswipe and the dexterously executed dollop of meager, pitying praise are all delightful. As your relationship to your peers and competitors matures and deepens, these can all be considered preludes to the final act. I refer, of course, to the "not-so-subtle" backstab.

With a proper attitude and an ego as large as the moon, you too can shred old businesses, fire workers in job lot packages, downsize, outsource and shift production overseas. You will not have had so much fun since you tied an M-80 to the tail of Aunt Hattie's cat.

Corporations are insane places. In corporate life, you only have to give the appearance of being a grown-up. Meanwhile, you will act out the fantasies that made life so charming when you were six. Want to be a pirate? Well, pull out the rubber cutlasses and run up the Jolly Roger. Al Dunlap and Carl Icahn did.

Corporate Lunacy

MEMORABLE EXECUTIVES AND WORKERS

"He is a modest little man who has a good deal to be modest about."
Sir Winston Churchill (1874-1965)

Numerous corporate inhabitants have, by their example, provided inspiration for this book. These people populated hundreds of companies I was exposed to during the twenty-five years I hung out in the corporate world. In order to protect their identities (and to keep me from getting my lights punched out), I developed a clever scheme to disguise them. The most memorable individuals were evaluated psychologically. This was done using the vast knowledge I garnered from three courses in psychology, postgraduate studies in an unrelated field and some painful real world experience. Pretty heady stuff, huh?

A diagnosis for each of those involved, along with their case numbers, has been listed on the next few pages. In some instances, the diagnosis fits multiple personalities...urrrh, people. You will note that those in charge are more bizarre than the worker-bees. These are all real people with some pretty grotesque (unreal) personalities. I have not made these people up! Without them, the corporation wouldn't be such a crazy place.

Introduction

MEMORABLE CORPORATE INMATES

Case Number	Diagnosis
1001	Can't distinguish between plans (fantasy) and results (reality).
1002	Schizoid psychopath. Will kill for a promotion.
1003-1033	MBA with delusions of grandeur (this may be redundant).
1034	Has deep-seated belief that accountants can have cosmic thoughts.
1035	Suffers from mindless order-taking disorder. Sheep complex.
1036	Fixated on appearance. Exhibits Ken & Barbie syndrome.
1037	Chronic attention deficit disorder. Can't focus on proper targets.
1038-1098	Compulsive agreement syndrome. Chronic yes man/person.
1099	Aggressive, repulsive jerk! Delusions of sexual attractiveness.
2000	Evidences autistic drive to make the simple become complex.

Corporate Lunacy

Case Number	Diagnosis
2001	Irrational need to attend conferences and seminars.
2002	Napoleonic control-freak disorder. Severe psychotic manipulator.
2003	Reality challenged. Never found a number he didn't like.
2004	Teamwork phobia. Doesn't play well with others.
2005	Harbors paranoid belief of a legal exposure in every situation.
2006	Has obsessive need for "state-of-the-art" financing.
2007	A catatonic prodigious ponderer. Results impaired.
2008	Fetish for creating policy manuals and mission statements.
2049-2055	Has neurotic need to wallow. Exhibits pigsty office syndrome.
2056	Preoccupied by use of consultants. Can't make a decision.
2057	Exhibits manic fetish to put a good face on results.

Introduction

Do you think you spot yourself on the list? If so, remember, "Recognition is the first step toward recovery." You will note that I'm not on the list. Why should it surprise you that I'm currently in denial?

Perhaps you bought this book to promote truth, understanding, apple pie and an awareness of the abuses of the modern corporation. Perhaps you bought this book so that my wife can shop for groceries in a supermarket rather than a pet store. Do I care?

Am I out to make a buck just like those other self-help authors? Of course I am. We can't beat the corporation, but at least we can laugh at the reality-challenged folks who run the place...I did. Maybe you can even find a way to leave early...I did. Let me show you how.

Introduction

Ralph was prepared!

Corporate Lunacy

1 BEGINNING CORPORATE LIFE

Sliding Into The Grind

Are you really crazy enough to enter corporate life? Apparently.

Let's stagger through the basics. First, you've got to get hired, right? There are interviews, in-your-face physicals and many other grinding introductory rituals to live through.

I guarantee that, after you have read this section, you'll be the best prepared corporate hopeful...i.e., dithering dolt...ever to take his/her shaky steps through the glass doors and up the shiny elevator to the great world of the modern corporation.

You'll learn how to survive that first terrible week and how to distinguish between temporary friends and immediate enemies.

Let's go get 'em, tiger.

THE INTERVIEW - Just Get A Job!

"Examinations are formidable even to the best prepared, for the greatest fool may ask more than the wisest man can answer."
Charles Caleb Colton (1780-1832)

If you don't already work for a big corporation, this chapter will give you hints on how to get a job. It may take some creativity (like lying about your credentials and your past), but what the heck.

If you now work for a corporation, you might recognize some of the things you did to land your current position. If you are one of the millions who were outsized, downsized, or simply wrong sized, you might wonder why you ever went down this path in the first place.

So you want to get on the fast track toward becoming Vice President in Charge of Major Stuff. Just by working hard you will gain power, prestige, play golf and make lots of money. NOT! If you believe that you are certainly Miss Naive Muffet. In reality, they will poke, prod, review, brainwash, socialize, indoctrinate, homogenize and normalize you until you have lost your individuality. You may spend your working life in total boredom. Or you may develop a bad case of hives.

Someday you will wonder why you didn't do something useful with your life like drink beer, ogle the girls/boys and play beach volleyball. Not convinced? Oh well, no turning back now. Let's go and get that job!

Your first step into the Acme Corporation is the interview...a required ritual for admittance. The interviewer is Marvin Wentworth-The Manager of Human Resources (HR). Not to worry! Wentworth is harmless.

Don't misunderstand me! There are value-added people in HR. They just happen to be as rare as condors. HRs are the poor lost souls that either failed in their last job or "ticked off" someone in charge. After all, why else would they be in HR?

Wentworth will pretend to have an interest in you, while you will pretend you're qualified for anything he might be looking for.

If you have written a typical resume, shame on you-your nose should be growing like Pinocchio's. You want him to believe that you've run several companies, graduated from college (with honors) and led several student organizations. You have traveled extensively and directed charities and youth groups.

In short, you are the most well-rounded individual since Dale Carnegie. You've now reached a state of perfection and wisdom. And to think you did all this before you turned twenty-two. Relax...Wentworth has really only skimmed your resume for a few key words anyway.

You probably don't interview well. So what? Most people don't. I suggest that you find someone to go in your place who will look good, be articulate and get the job. Strongly consider hiring a professional actor. After all, would you hire the real, boring and unimaginative you? Wentworth won't remember whom he interviewed when you arrive for work on your first day. It's just sad that you can't find someone to work in your place for the next thirty years as well.

That said, you'll probably insist on doing the interview yourself (with all the risk that entails). OK, if you must, remember that you only have about a half-hour to make a good impression. Don't talk about yourself, you egomaniac. Get Wentworth to talk about the only thing he finds really fascinating...himself. Remember to maintain good eye contact as he pours out his soul. Wentworth will be asking a number of stock questions that he has asked in every interview he has done over the last thirty-five years. To get the job, you need to answer the right way. He will ask:

1. **"Are you highly intelligent?"** You shouldn't appear to be. If you are intelligent, you are a potential trouble maker. You will probably make waves and create work.

2. **"Are you pliable?"** Your answer should be YES. Get used to this. If hired, you will be getting lots of pliability practice.

3. **"Are you willing to work long hours?"** Of course you are. You are willing to work more hours than there are in a day.

4. **"Do you have broad interests?"** This is easy. The answer is NO! Acme Corporation wants production. They don't want someone who has a life.

5. **"Do you know anything about the company?"** Of

Corporate Lunacy

course! Your grandfather, your mother and all your living relatives buy its products. You have wanted to work here since before you were born.

6. **"Are you a people person?"** Careful here, this is a trick! Wentworth wants to find out if you will spend all your time yakking! Your answer should be: "I would be a people person if I allowed myself any time. However, I never talk or associate with people during work. On the weekends, I'm usually in the office."

7. **"What are your goals?"** Your answer is, "I hope to be Chairperson someday; however, I'm willing to start in the mailroom and hope to have the privilege of working in Human Resources. I would hope I could work with you as my mentor." (This seems like obvious sucking up, but if Wentworth is your average HR professional, he won't recognize that.)

8. **"What salary are you looking for?"** Tell him that you would be willing to work for the experience, but you need to earn money to support your crippled mother and meet your charitable giving goals. You will settle for whatever seems fair.

Wentworth will probably also ask some off-the-wall questions just to see how you will react. The little weasel wants to make you squirm. For example, he may ask: "Why is a manhole cover round?" Then, "If you were ice cream, what flavor would you be?"

React vigorously! Calmly inform Mister Wentworth that you don't answer inane, trick questions. Tell him that recent EEO guidelines suggest severe penalties for this type of harassment. You will find at this point that he will want to limit his losses by offering you a job. Take it!

Now wasn't that easy? You didn't overwork your conscience. Marvin Wentworth is not likely to check your references (that would involve work). You've got the job assuming you can pass the pre-employment physical. Wasn't that your goal?

THE PRE-EMPLOYMENT PHYSICAL – Proper Etiquette

"My doctor gave me six months to live, but when I couldn't pay the bill, he gave me six months more."
Walter Matthau (1920-2000)

So you passed your interview. Didn't I tell you that you would? Now, the only ordeal between you and your first day on the job is the dreaded pre-employment physical. You are destined to have an encounter of the closest kind with the company physician.

You must use decorum, obey high standards of conduct and observe proper etiquette during the pre-employment physical. Unfortunately, no one has written a book on proper manners during the physical. You can't just pick up a copy of Amy Vanderbilt and find the guidance you need for this situation. Therefore, this chapter fills the information void with a few practical etiquette tips. So, mind your manners and your derriere.

Make a good first impression on the doctor and his assistants. He will tell you men to strip down to your skivvies. Jockey shorts make a more favorable impression than a leopard skin thong.

The jewelry around your neck should weigh less than your shoes. Perfume, if any, should be a masculine fragrance, rather than a fufu floral spray. Consider trimming your hair rather than tying it back in a ponytail.

For you ladies, your makeup should weigh less than your clothes. A demure Maidenform bra is preferable to the spiked leather harness that you wear at home. Display an appropriate level of modesty. It is unseemly for a lady to ask the doctor if he likes the butterfly tattoo on her breast. Describing in exhaustive detail how you got that full suntan with no tan lines is likewise inappropriate. It is wholly improper to describe how that poison ivy found its way to your derriere.

As for you macho men...recognize that bragging about your "equipment" is certainly not good manners.

Observe a high standard of decency regarding personal hygiene. It is clearly bad form to leave that green fungus under your toenails. Eating a garlic sandwich before the exam is just plain gross and may cause the doctor distress.

If you have jogged five miles and lifted weights for an hour, decorum suggests a shower. Be observant...if the physician wears a gas mask during the exam, this may indicate that your hygiene is in need of attention.

Chapter 1 - Beginning Corporate Life

Some key points of etiquette to heed during the exam —

- **Your Medical History.** They will ask you to fill out a form with questions about your medical history. The proper answer to the sex question is "male" or "female." Answers such as "not often enough" or "really swell" are not acceptable.
- **The Gown.** Why do they always give you a gown that doesn't fit? The damned thing is either a tent that a Sumo wrestler could wear or something too small for a Leprechaun. And how do you tie that stupid thing behind your back? Just do the best you can.
- **The Height and Weight Check.** Is it acceptable to put lifts in your socks when they check your height? Of course! Adding a couple of inches to your height mutes that weight problem. The doctor will nevertheless conclude that you are overweight...unless you are certifiably anorexic.
- **The Blood Test.** The nurse will undoubtedly try to fill two quart-sized Mason jars with your blood. You should graciously submit to this procedure. They need all that blood because there weren't enough winos at the blood bank. It is insensitive to ask if they are getting a kickback.
- **The Lung Capacity Check.** The nurse is not looking for a world-class ten-second belch when she says, "We want to check your lung capacity."
- **The Hearing Test.** They will put you in a soundproof booth and tell you to push a button every time you hear

a sound. What if your ears are ringing because you have a hangover from the party last night? Deportment requires that you should not push the button every other second just for the fun of it. (Type A individuals, with a need to score, are the only ones to pass the hearing test anyway.)

- **The Urine Test.** They will tell you to fill the cup to the line. However, you are so nervous that you can only dribble. What should you do? Politeness requires that you fill the cup as they have requested. It is permissible to use any liquid available, including tap water. You may consider using other lab samples, if available. However, recognize the risk that you may have chosen a drug-positive sample.

- **The Hernia Examination.** Men...At some point during the exam you will be standing there wearing nothing but a smile and some paper slippers. The doctor will grab your crotch with his cold hands; tell you to turn your head; jam his fingers still deeper; and tell you to cough. Cough...hell! It feels like he's trying to neuter you...without any anesthetic. Remember to maintain an atmosphere of quiet dignity. Shrieks, screams and curses are signs of poor upbringing.

- **The Sigmoid Scope.** Propriety suggests that you not giggle during the rectal examination or request a "do-over." You may be tempted to bring your own teddy bear (so that you can relax). This is not considered good manners. Would you bring your own food when invited to an important dinner? The doctor will be offended if you don't use his teddy bear. And do not be so boorish as to tell the doctor it feels like he's jammed fifty feet of garden hose up your butt.

You must be gracious even under the most embarrassing of circumstances. For example, what if you step off the exam table and slip? With your gown around your ears you slide across the room into the wall, almost knocking over the nurse in the process. With dignity, pick yourself up and say something clever, such as: "Isn't it fun to play sled?"

If you are so obese that the exam table gets caught between your cheeks, just comment, "This must be the slim line version." During the exam, if you find that you are giving the window washer a full frontal view, you might consider saying, "I find it important to establish a bond with the little people."

So, before we say bon voyage...when you Type A managers find your posterior in the air waiting for the Sigmoidoscopy: Good manners and your survival suggest that you don't take this moment to make abusive demands of the doctor. And this is not the time to discuss your thoughts about how the company could reduce costs by "downsizing" the medical department.

ON THE JOB – Your First Few Days

"I always pass on good advice. It is the only thing to do with it. It is never of any use to oneself."
Oscar Wilde (1854-1900)

You arrived early at Acme Corporate headquarters for your first day of work, full of enthusiasm about your new job. You knew that this first week might be critical to your success. Optimistic? You bet! After all, they hired you because they thought you were a winner, didn't they?

Of course, the guards frisked you at the gate. Oh well, you aren't a VIP yet. You signed in and waited patiently in the

First day?

Chapter 1 - Beginning Corporate Life

lobby. You stared with admiration at the pictures of former Acme Chairmen that adorned the walls. You swelled with pride as they issued you your very own temporary badge designating you as a new Acme employee.

Wentworth (the HR guy who interviewed you) finally appeared. How good it was to see a familiar face...a comrade...a fellow worker. Curious...he didn't seem to remember you at all. Now, now. No time to get overly sensitive. He gave you that canned speech about how Acme Corporation is a great place to work. You felt a real bond.

You filled out a mountain of forms enthusiastically: employment forms, tax forms, social security forms, life insurance forms, beneficiary forms, payroll forms...forms and more forms. Gosh, what a wonderfully thorough company Acme is.

Wentworth gave you a lecture on the things that could get you fired: conflict of interest, revealing company secrets, discrimination policy violations, lies on your resume, misappropriation of company resources, insubordination...to name a few.

You thought: "They use those policies to screen out problem employees. That's how Acme is able to maintain such a first-class team." Wentworth issued you your very own copy of the Employee Manual. You were now officially on the Acme team. Wow...I mean...like WOW!

Your new boss Warren Flingabout's secretary Betty escorted you to an empty office. She said, "Make yourself comfortable,

Mr. Flingabout will be with you shortly." Then she gave you some material to read and left. You eagerly checked out your surroundings. What a neat new office they had given you...a 15x20-foot corner office with windows, burled wood, nice potted plants and a large desk. You were just beginning to settle in when Betty came to tell you that your real office was ready. She led you to your new home – a 5x5 cubicle with excellent access (adjacent) to the men's room. It was much nicer than the one you saw next to the dumpster.

Flingabout appeared. He was exceptionally well dressed, confident, articulate and knowledgeable. He warned you about the need to fit in. "Cultivate a thoughtful image by reserving judgment until you understand the needs of the organization," he said.

Then he told you about the experience of some guy named Conners. "Bill Conners came to the Acme Corporation from GE. He criticized Acme's planning approach as being ad hoc. He said, 'At GE, we planned our work and then worked our plan.' Nobody wanted to hear that trite crap. He was branded a nitpicker, obsessed with form, not substance. The guy lasted about six months before he got the axe. Check with me before you go out on a limb." Gosh, this guy really knew his stuff.

He also told you to observe the standards of dress at Acme. Let's see...the executives all wear Brooks Brothers' suits, silk club ties and black wingtip shoes. Looked as if you could contribute your Kmart wardrobe to the thrift store.

Flingabout actually sat down for five minutes and gave

you the benefit of his long experience. Looked as if he was the kind of boss you could really bond with.

Well, you worked for Flingabout for less than two months. One day he was gone. No one seemed to know where. It had something to do with "personal reasons." Apparently, Flingabout was not a good choice as a mentor.

Flingabout's demise was not fatal to your career, but it sure put a damper on things. Was there something you didn't notice about Flingabout? I should think so!

To improve your perception powers, I have constructed the following little quiz. Test your skill. Determine which of the following people would make a good choice as mentor.

MOVER AND SHAKER QUIZ

1. **Ed Markey...**Nice guy, straightforward, team builder. Did not engage in political maneuvering. Produced consistent business results. Took personal responsibility for the results of his business.

2. **Lester Forsythe...**He thought describing a problem was the same as solving it. Had finger on pulse of office politics. Could paint believable pictures of the future.

3. **J. Pennington Nicely...**He had a very inquisitive mind and many ideas for the business. A whirling dervish of energy. He created a job for himself, but also created needless work for others.

4. **Brent Hardcover**...Arrogant and abusive. Quick with the reprimand. Never in doubt, but often wrong. Nicknamed "pit bull." Eliminated anyone who questioned his authority.
5. **Warren Flingabout**...Immaculate dresser, articulate, confident and knowledgeable.

So let's see how you did. If you chose anyone but Forsythe you flunked. You are headed for a short career. All the others were fired, demoted or transferred to obscure outposts.

RIGHT   **Forsythe** – was non-threatening and ego boosting to Welbly, the CEO. Forsythe was a keeper.

WRONG   **Markey** – Was held personally responsible for a sales downturn caused by an economic recession. Now Supervisor-Forms Management.

WRONG   **Nicely** – Originally hired because of his energy and initiative. Because of his million questions...just a pain. Transferred to subsidiary in Butte, Montana.

WRONG   **Hardcover** – Tried to downsize CEO's nephew and quickly found himself a rightsizing victim. I wonder if they tortured him before they canned his butt.

WRONG   **Flingabout** – Were you paying attention? He's gone. Fired! He embarrassed himself in front of the Board. They thought he was mostly BS, not much substance. A highly educated moron. He cared more about travel plans than business plans. Now a consultant.

Some other thoughts on your first few days.

You probably thought you were in it for the long haul. Kind of a ridiculous notion. Today, no one keeps their job very long. If you shoot yourself in the foot, don't expect bandages or a chance to redeem yourself. So what the heck, you might as well enjoy however long you have left.

Chapter 1 - Beginning Corporate Life

Ralph could see himself as management material.

Corporate Lunacy

2 YOUR MISSION, SHOULD YOU CHOOSE TO ACCEPT IT

Adjusting

Adjust, adjusting, adjusted, to be adjusted, not maladjusted, very adjusted, getting more adjusted day by day, so adjusted that they could use you for a carpenter's level if the building started to tilt. Look closely now…watch this bright light…do you see it, concentrate, keep watching…your eyelids are getting heavy, they're starting to close, you're getting very, very adjusted, and you will be adjusted for ever and ever…

WALK THE WALK – Talk the Talk

"We have to put things in such a way as to make people who would otherwise hang us, believe we are joking."
George Bernard Shaw (1856-1950)

This is a quiz! Where does how you look, what you say and how you say it matter more than what you do? There are three right answers: The Miss America Contest, politics and the modern corporation.

Ever notice how many executives are narcissistic mirror gazers? They always say just the right thing and they seem so proactive. However, when it comes right down to it, can you figure out what they really do? Should you despise them? Heck no! You might want to emulate them. Picture yourself getting promoted, having lots of money and playing low-handicap golf. Why does it matter that your net contribution to business is about as significant as a sparrow fart?

Observe how the executives dress. They have religiously studied John Molloy's Dress for Success. They do not wear polyester suits. Their pure wool suits will be gray, dark blue or black, thank you. Solid or very conservative stripes (bold stripes are for gangsters, not for the aspiring businessperson).

Do I even have to tell you not to wear a brown or green suit? Ties are to be made of silk...rayon or polyester is out. Shirts will be 100 percent cotton (only blue or white, please). Use either a button-down or tab collar.

Corporate Lunacy

Shoes will be black or cordovan, wing tips or plain lace-ups. Lose those cowboy boots. Socks for the men will be black and extend to the knee. Fishnet hose is not acceptable for the ladies. The belt will be black, conservative and new.

You will note that this is how the boss dresses. If your boss is Bill Gates or Steven Jobs and he wears jeans and tee shirts to work, forget all this other stuff. The cardinal rule of attire is to dress like the boss…he wants to see himself without having to go to the mirror in the executive washroom.

I don't know about you, but I always went home at the end of the day with my shirt wrinkled and my pants rumpled. In contrast, upwardly mobile Steve Bowler looked as if he had just come from the tailor and the manicurist. Every crease was in place. How did he do that? The starch on his shirts was so heavy that it would take a Sumo wrestler to wrinkle them. Did he ever sit down? Maybe he had a steamer in the bottom drawer of his desk. Never a hair out of place…not even one.

Oh well, let's get back to what you need to do. Men, you need to see if Clinton's or Michael Douglas's barber has any open time on his appointment book. Use enough hair tonic to hold down a Ferris wheel…and no facial hair.

Women should also take note. Bleach that mustache, gals! No hairstyles that look like they came from a food processor. Accessories should include horn rimmed glasses, a proper conservative watch but no heavy gold jewelry.

Now you've got it! You look the part! Basically, you look like the total dork that you have become, but you're now executive material.

Okay, so let's move on to that talking stuff. If you want to be upwardly mobile, you must sound important even if you have nothing to say. You'll have to master the skill of bureaucratic double-speak. Mumble intelligently and with sincerity. Try some of the following which demonstrate the point. These are taken from real business communications:

1. "We are aligning internal metrics with customer expectations." This means they will change what they do to match what the customer wants.

2. "We have aligned people resources to accelerate inquiry closure." Translation...they have put some people in customer service who have enough brains to answer your questions.

3. "We are leveraging technology to capture and share authorization information across our business." They will begin talking with each other.

Learn to speak of core competencies, pacing technologies and leveraging protectable technologies. Prattle about synergies, leadership position, share momentum, holistic value and Economic Value Added.

Pontificate about pay-for-performance, diversity training, multiculturalism, affirmative action and self-actualization. Finally, throw in a few acronyms for good measure: MIPs,

QUIPs, EVA, OIRONCE, MVA, ROI, ROE, RONA, FASB, LIFO, GAAP and FIFO.

Of course, all this stuff is a smoke screen for not having anything of value to say. If you really wanted to be understood you would eschew obfuscation and begin elucidating in comprehensible prose. Whew!

It helps to have a deep booming voice that demands attention. If yours is high and squeaky...take voice lessons. Use that voice at the right time and say the appropriate things.

If you have any thoughts of your own...Get rid of them! Just paraphrase what your boss says. Sit attentively. Wait for those pregnant pauses. Then reflectively say, "Let me summarize where we are." If the boss asks you a direct question – caaaarrefulllll! State with deep conviction, "I think whatever it is that you think."

Keep your desk clean! Only geeks, techies and lower-level managers have more than one small neat pile on their desk. Delegate! There's always someone around who really likes to work.

Always appear busy, but don't do anything tangible. It is easier to criticize the work of others than to produce results of your own.

Always be on the way to an important meeting, "Too busy to stop, write me a memo." Of course the golf course qualifies as a meeting. Am I going too fast here? You're going "off-site," aren't you?

You might try to emulate Steve Bowler. Steve got promotion after promotion, though he never really mastered any job he ever had.

Steve was good looking, socially astute, smart and had a confident-sounding, deep, resonant voice. He could spout all the leading-edge buzzwords. He sucked up to the right people by mirroring what they said.

He always seemed to work on the high-profile projects. He was blue-blooded, patrician, lazy and suave. He took credit for others' ideas and work. Above all, he had a Teflon coating. (Too bad that Steve recently disappeared.)

So, don't gamble on your grooming; appear in appropriate apparel; and practice your paraphrasing. What else do you have to do? Have you been paying attention? You are to do nothing, nada! Sit back, without rumpling your Armani, and let those promotions roll in.

BE A TEAM PLAYER – Happy Talk.

"Men stumble over the truth from time to time, but most pick themselves up and hurry off as if nothing happened."
Winston Churchill (1874-1965)

If you want to get ahead in the corporation, you must learn to be a team player. This is another way of saying that you must agree with everything the boss says. You must learn to do this with style, grace and creativity. Ingrain these skills until they are habits and your agreement, compulsive.

So, what's wrong with a little flattery, fawning and good

old-fashioned sucking up? What's wrong with happy, happy, happy talk?

Did your boss ever ask you for your honest opinion on something he did? Did you give it to him? If you did, are you enjoying your unemployment? Let's assume you don't have a cognitive disorder. If so, you can acquire the skills needed to be a corporate yes-man/person…a real team player.

Some of the words for the proficiency you seek to develop may seem harsh. Your coworkers might call you a brown-nose, sycophant, suck-up, yes-man, yes-person, spineless flatterer, fawner, flunky, adulator, parasite, bootlick, kissass, toady or a sniveler. Is that so bad? Courage now…sticks and stones, etc.

Fitting in might be a challenge.

Chapter 2 - Your Mission, Should You Choose to Accept It

After all, do you want to be liked by the boss, receive promotions, make a lot of money and be put on the list for a bunch of perks; or do you want friends? Why are you hesitating? You don't need friends at work. In fact, "friends" at work is an oxymoron.

See what happens to those friends if you are downsized. See how long it takes them to acquire your desk, artwork and computer. You can always buy a dog if you need a friend. You will find a dog to be more reliable.

It is always disconcerting when the people you are trying to "suck up" to don't have time for you. That's because they are trying to "suck up" to the people above them.

What can be effective is the indirect suck-up. Position yourself within earshot of the target of your flattery. Speak in a loud voice, raving about the benefits of having such a wonderful boss.

Think ahead in your career and target someone higher-up in the corporation, perhaps your boss's boss, and perfect the side-step suck-up. You must be careful to keep your present boss from being annoyed. If your present boss is within earshot, you might try something like, "My boss tells me frequently that he stands in awe of you." This may earn you double points as a twin-tower suck-up.

You should also master indirect ways of sucking up. First, consider generous use of the gatekeeper suck-up. This involves running errands for the boss's secretary. Appropriate fawning behavior and presents will help assure that she makes favorable mention of you. Be careful, however; this technique is so obvious, and so many of your colleagues will be doing it, that you must be skillful.

The spousal suck-up can be very effective but must be employed carefully. If the boss can't stand his wife, getting on her good side may not be helpful. If she thinks you are trying to proposition her, instead of just enlisting her support, you will have big trouble.

Think about the medium of the message. There are many opportunities to perfect the oral suck-up (It's not what you think, but consider all the options). Of course, in these days of the computer, you should consider the e-mail suck-up. The latter gives you a chance to get your message of devotion out to all the troops. I don't recommend e-mail, however, if you are hypersensitive to negative feedback from your coworkers.

An excellent place to demonstrate that you are a real team player is the committee meeting. Committees don't reach conclusions, make decisions or accomplish much. Instead, they allow executives to analyze, ponder, mull, cogitate, deliberate, meditate and contemplate until the problem goes away. So be enthusiastic as the committee is split into sub-committees, task forces and working groups.

Let's say that you are appointed to a high impact committee to reduce office supplies or to rewrite the corporate policy manual. If your boss is present, committees can be excellent forums for the charming little echo suck-up.

Listen attentively, and whenever your boss makes a statement, immediately paraphrase what he said. All bosses

49

enjoy this! While they love to hear themselves speak, it is even more gratifying to hear an echo of their thoughts coming from somebody else.

It is deplorable that you must learn all these skills in on-the-job training. Unfortunately, colleges don't have courses in Flattery 101. I recommend that you observe and emulate master yes-persons. Fortunately, you will find numerous role models in the modern corporation.

THE YES-MAN/PERSON HALL OF FAME

1. **Ollie North** – He said nothing that could be viewed as contrary.
2. **All US vice-presidents** – It's their job!
3. **Hitler's generals** – "We were just following orders."
4. **Johnny Framer** – That little twerp in the front row in high school English.
5. **George Stephanopoulos** – His picture's in Webster's Illustrated Dictionary under sycophant.
6. **Judge Ito** – He was in charge but thought he had to please both sides.
7. **Brutus** – I think Caesar may have misjudged a bit, don't you?
8. **All lawyers and most accountants**.
9. **All real estate and insurance brokers**.
10. **All appearance freaks** – It goes with the territory.

Corporate Lunacy

Remember that you're trying to get ahead in the corporation. It takes energy and is suicide to dispute the boss. Why not learn to suck-up...go with the flow? The boss will consider you to be a real team player. It's time for happy, happy, happy talk.

COMMAND PERFORMANCE – the Boss's Party.

"Enjoying myself?...Certainly, there is nothing else here to enjoy."
George Bernard Shaw (1856-1950)

Remember when Leland Oberstar (the boss) invited you and your wife to that first horrid Christmas party at his house? It may have sounded like fun if you'd never been to one of his command performances.

The guy actually thought that his employees wanted to be there, but he was delusional. I, for one, would rather endure a double hernia than suffer through another such party...ever!

One reason Oberstar had these parties was because the company paid all the expense. He used these parties to supplement his normal living expense. His wife froze all the excess food. He ordered twice as much wine as was needed then cellared anything that was left over for his personal consumption.

Oberstar was the host...so I guess the rest of you were just unwilling parasites. He was also a crashing bore. Don't tell me you really enjoyed the elaborate descriptions he gave of his prowess at flower arranging.

You arrived on time for the party. So far, so good! You had memorized a few social do's and don'ts. You hugged the hostess, even though she wore that awful, but expensive, perfume. This was entirely proper.

Jane introduced herself to your wife for the third year in a row and commented that she didn't believe they'd met. You noted that your wife seemed to want to strangle Jane. You also noted that this may be a sign that you're not upwardly mobile.

You wanted to assure that this command performance was not your last, so you didn't tell Jane that her eclectic taste in furniture was bizarre. You also didn't comment to Oberstar that his wife's new spiked haircut looked like a butch biker's. Actually, she looked a lot like Susan Powter, on a bad hair day. Dinner, as always, represented an opportunity for some major league social errors. First, there was the seating arrangement at the table. They put you next to Ernie the office dweeb. Hmmm...This was probably another sign that the Presidency was out of reach. Ernie was a social disaster. At least you didn't laugh at his jokes.

The food was catered and awful. Thank goodness you didn't tell the host that the paté looked like Spam and tasted like cat food. The main course was some unidentifiable meat. "Looks like chicken, but it's too small...maybe it's roadkill," you thought.

Oberstar proudly announced that the wine was the oldest in his collection. You carefully avoided putting ice cubes in it. This was good. Plus, you knew not to test the wine by gargling.

The dinner conversation offered some real opportunities to embarrass yourself, so you wisely chose to remain in the background. This party was not the place to demonstrate the animal noises which were such a hit at frat parties. Likewise, you thought it best not to mention that you once took Oberstar's daughter to a frat "pig" party and won the ugly-date contest.

Have you noticed that every office party has a Ken and Barbie couple? They planned their whole night in excruciating detail – who sucks up to whom and when, etc. They researched the boss's ethnic origins to determine whether or not to laugh at certain stories. They feigned genuine interest in Oberstar's passionate preoccupation with croquet. They delighted in his daughter's recent ballet performance. They seemed fascinated when Jane explained her homemade yogurt. They were empathetic about her recent gall bladder operation.

Ken and Barbie made the other guests nauseous. They were first to stand when Jane led everyone in a Texas line dance. While your wife joined the dance, you quietly went to the master bathroom and heaved your dinner into the Jacuzzi.

The evening never seemed to end. Oberstar thought it would be swell for everyone to stand around the piano and sing Christmas carols. Jane played...badly. "Isn't this fun?" said Oberstar. Ken and Barbie raved about Jane's piano artistry.

Should you have been more conspicuous? I don't think so. You survived. What more do you want? If you had performed too well, Oberstar might have invited you to be his personal guest at the ballet. He invited Ken and Barbie. Sometimes being too successful results in a heavy price to pay.

For future reference, here's some advice about the boss's party:

1. **Your attendance is required.** Can you believe that some people actually think that these affairs are optional? If you have another commitment, cancel it. A conflict with the bowling league awards banquet is not a valid reason to skip the party. Some people use the excuse that a relative died. If you try this, remember that your Aunt Mimi can only die once.

Once there, choose one of the following approaches to get through the evening:

2. **Be inconspicuous.** Try to blend into the background like a piece of furniture. This is clearly the safe approach. Just observe some elementary etiquette. A party at the boss's house requires somewhat different manners than a party at the local truckers' bar.

3. **Be a brilliant conversationalist.** If this appeals to you, consider getting a book on clever things to say at social gatherings. Speak in sonorous, self-important tones filled with apparent wisdom. Liberally drop names of important people and exotic places. Pontificate at length on Chinese affairs based on the vast expertise gained in the three days you recently spent there. Your coworkers will despise you, but the boss will adore you.

4. **Be creative.** It's not possible to avoid these things altogether. However, consider showing up but then becoming violently ill in front of everyone. They will gladly send you home.

PERFORMANCE TARGETS – If You Can't Hit Them, Redefine Them!

"He uses statistics as a drunken man uses lamp-posts – for support rather than illumination."
Andrew Lang (1844-1912)

If you were compensated for action rather than talk you might not get that fat bonus. So what if you spent more time on the golf course than working at your desk? If you failed to meet your goals because things just didn't go very well, would that be fair? Of course not! You have a right to make those big bucks, even if your performance doesn't measure up.

Management often thinks of low profits and unmet quotas as signs of failure. Don't submit. If you don't like those numbers, redefine them. We're not talking about anything dishonest here, like lies. Rather, we are concerned with a very simple skill – information management – making things look good that would otherwise look bad.

Consider the example of Elmer Stockman, Production Manager for the Gears and Bolts Corporation. Elmer had been delivering reports to management about (and his bonus was based on) worker productivity. This is a concept he expressed as pounds of production per man-hour.

His results were always on target (as long as he ignored the scrap rate that had increased from 3 to 28 percent). Of course, it was easy to produce more pounds, because the market continued to shift toward larger, heavier gears.

Unfortunately, pounds per man-hour had recently begun to slip. Worse, Stockman was getting heat from an unsympathetic management that was more concerned about profit than excuses.

So Stockman did a thorough financial analysis of the problem. He examined his need for an income to support his wife's expensive tastes. He computed his son's car payments and evaluated his daughter's worthless husband. He also contemplated his package of executive perks, including country club membership and company auto.

Corporate Lunacy

The analysis revealed the obvious: THE NUMBERS MUST BE REDEFINED! Inspiration came to Stockman. "If we can't hit the target," he said, "we'll just change it to one we can."

Stockman concluded that the historical trend of pounds per man-hour was useless, because this statistic gave the wrong impression. Actual pounds per man-hour compared to budgeted pounds per man-hour didn't look good. Therefore, some adjustments needed to be made.

Because pounds per man-hour moved up and down with levels of production, budgets should be adjusted for this change. They also needed to be adjusted for changes in product mix and seasonality, excluding overtime and non first-class production while compensating for depreciation of equipment. Finally, a subjective measure, relating to the "feel" of the numbers, was employed to come up with "adjusted pounds per man-hour."

After Stockman made this change, pounds per man-hour (redefined) rose every year. There were none of the bothersome dips and valleys found in the original data. For simplicity, Stockman referred to "adjusted pounds per man-hour" as "pounds per man-hour." Ahhh! This is the stuff from which full bonus payouts are made.

Stockman's golf game continued to improve because he could now spend more time on the golf course. Stockman's wife sustained her previous spending pattern, and his son continued to receive his support. Too bad company profits fell. Well, you can't have everything.

When Stockman retired, the Gears and Bolts Corporation promoted his daughter's worthless husband to Manager of Production. This poor guy actually thought that pounds per man-hour meant pounds per man-hour. He didn't do any of the creative adjustments necessary to make bad numbers look good.

After a disheartening year in the old man's seat, he was fired. Stockman's daughter, in her divorce suit, told the judge that her daddy had been right about him all along!

Let's learn a little something from Stockman, okay? Actual performance is not as important as perceived performance. People want to feel good, and it's a bummer when the numbers are bad. It's your responsibility to protect your emotionally fragile fellow executives from a bruising encounter with reality. Therefore, learn to redefine.

GETTING PAST THE GATEKEEPER

"I've always been interested in people, but I've never liked them."
W. Somerset Maugham (1874-1965)

It's Monday morning and that important contract you have been negotiating is finally coming to fruition. You need to see Stubblefield (the Senior Executive Vice President of Finance) in the next few days to assure that he is comfortable with the deal. There is some urgency because your competitors are also working hard to land this account. If Stubblefield doesn't sign-off before the weekend, they'll probably get the contract instead of you.

Guarding the way to Stubblefield's office is Ms. Robbins, his personal secretary. They call her the gatekeeper. All top executives have one. Trying to get information from one is like trying to get a straight answer from a politician. Provoke her and she can be as vicious as a Rottweiler guarding a junkyard.

Optimistically, you pick up the phone and dial Stubblefield's office. Your conversation probably goes something like this:

Ms. Robbins answers, "Mr. Stubblefield's office."

You inquire hopefully, "Is he there? I need to talk to him."

She says, "He's in a meeting. He is not available."

You say, "This is extremely important."

A frosty silence. Then, "May I leave Mr. Stubblefield a message?" She has used the dreaded words for the first time.

You say, "Could you have him call me?"

Ms. Robbins says curtly, "I can leave a message for him."

So you leave a rather lengthy message stressing your urgent need to speak with him. You wait anxiously in your office until 7:00 p.m. hoping that he will call you. Of course, he doesn't. You call again. Ms. Robbins is still there. "Oh," she says, "Mr. Stubblefield left hours ago. I will tell him you called." Note that she hasn't promised he will respond. She really hasn't promised anything at all. As far as you know, she will leave him a message at the bottom of her wastebasket.

Chapter 2 - Your Mission, Should You Choose to Accept It

Tuesday begins much the same way as Monday. You call with a concerned air and try to express the urgency of your position. You inquire politely whether Stubblefield might be able to return your call. You get the same response: "I'll leave him a message." Does she have any idea whether your need is a priority? Do you think she cares? The day ends with a gathering sense of gloom.

Wednesday is more of the same. You have now left ten telephone messages. Each time you hear the horrible, "May I take a message?" You begin to fret that he may never call you back. You have this sickening feeling that he may not even know you have been calling.

Suddenly, you have an inspiration. Why not call when the gatekeeper's out to lunch or after office hours? Maybe then you could talk to him directly. He might pick up the phone himself. Are you kidding me?

When Ms. Robbins is not there, her answering machine takes the call. You still can't reach him and she's the one that takes the messages off the answering machine. She types the ones she wants to give him. He never sees the others. You want to cry but decide to go drink instead.

It's Thursday morning and you are beginning to get desperate. So, what can you do? You try a different tack. You try to schedule a meeting with Stubblefield. What does she have to say about that? What do you expect? No can do!

She tells you firmly, "His calendar is very busy."

You push anxiously, "Can't I talk to him to see if he wants to see me?"

She says testily, "I'll give him the message."

Don't you just want to scream? Brunnehilde, the Norse Warrior-Princess, guards the gate.

Your frayed nerves indicate how little time is left. How can you get past the gatekeeper? A desperate but brilliant idea comes to mind. Why don't you just go to his office? You can hover expectantly outside his door. Then you can see for yourself whether or not he's there. Of course, sitting at the desk guarding the way to his office is Ms. Robbins. Seeing you, she gets up and closes his door. The sound rings in your ears: "I'll give him the message."

By Thursday afternoon, panic is setting in. You think, I'll sneak up there after she leaves. Right! Ms. Robbins' life is her job. She works far more hours than Stubblefield does. Dejectedly, you leave the office. It's like an awful jingle: "I'll leave him a message...I'll leave him a message...I'll leave him a message..."

Friday morning. You arrive very early. You'll get there before the gatekeeper arrives. Fat chance, Charlie. Of course she's already there. Probably sleeps there. It's just plain hopeless. She's in charge and you're not.

How will this story end? Most likely the day will end and you still will not have seen him. You don't know whether or not he ever got any of your messages. According to Ms. Robbins, he's always in a meeting. He's never available for you. Your competitors will get the contract, and you will get chewed out. What can you do? Not much.

There is a better way to handle Ms. Robbins. It won't help you this time, but it can save you in the future. It's really very simple. The word is preparation. Prepare the way long before you need something. Start a plan to get the gatekeeper on your side. Bond with her now. Here's how:

1. **Treat her as your superior.** She is, you know, regardless of her title.
2. **Bring her candy.** Remember the apple for the teacher? And not just any chocolates, you cheapskate. Neuhaus imported from Belgium is the only choice.
3. **Flowers are always a nice touch.** Get to know a good florist. You'll be using him often.
4. **Ask her advice.** Sit attentively at her feet as she dispenses wisdom.
5. **Write her notes of appreciation.**

Find out about her personal interests. Befriend her. Join her church. Sing in her choir. Make her laugh. Avoid ever being abrasive. Commit yourself energetically to the task. Bond as closely as you can and you never need to go through Hell Week again.

Corporate Lunacy

Management Boot Camp – A Modest Proposal

"I'm not going to rearrange the deck chairs on the Titanic."
Rogers Morton (1914-79)

America is losing its competitive edge but not for the reasons you think. It's because we've fallen under the spell of management consultants who sell books, seminars, presentations and courses exhorting us to be the enlightened managers we are not and never can be.

Anxious managers spend countless hours and over $20 billion per year on these programs where the success rate is the same as for fad diets...about five percent. For the other ninety-five percent, regression and despair follow temporary results.

It's like asking Yanni to play the piano like Van Cliburn, or Slim Whitman to sing an aria like Pavarotti. Yet some silly dolts actually buy this stuff.

Let's look at some of the things the management gurus are teaching and see why they don't produce the desired results:

Assertiveness Training. Do you really think that timid people can become assertive just because they are told to? "Uhhhh...pardon me sir, would it be too much to ask you not to hurt me while I try to convince you to do something you really don't want to do...if you're OK with that, of course?" Mr. Rogers can't become Henry Kravis just by reading a book.

63

Decision-Making Skills. Bias for action...Give me a break. What does teaching decision-making skills do for people who are afraid to make mistakes? You guessed it. It just gives them anxiety, guilt and an ulcer.

Empowerment and Leadership Skills. Now here's a really foolish craze. How many people are really capable of being leaders? Most people want to be followers. "You go ahead...I'm right behind you."

Sensitivity Training. Abusive managers don't become sensitive after they've taken sensitivity training. They just learn that before they tell you what a dog you are, they should always begin by saying: "I don't mean this to sound critical." Helpful, isn't it?

And what about those programs advocating better understanding between coworkers? When you really know what's going on inside Steve's head, do you love him more? Of course not! What you've now discovered was that your instinctive desire to punch his lights out was right on the money.

And then there are all those books that use stupid metaphors to impart their questionable wisdom. Do you really think management insights can be drawn from Winnie the Pooh, fishing stories, kindergarten, Homer's Iliad, Attila the Hun or Zen warriors?

Pity the poor souls that take this stuff seriously and do

Corporate Lunacy

themselves and their careers irreparable harm.

OK, you say, "All you do is criticize. Don't you have any answers?" Of course I do!

MANAGEMENT BOOT CAMP IS THE ANSWER.

Let the Marines run it. They can make you a man! Tear you down and then build you up again. Replace all those unacceptable habits with true management discipline. "On your knees, you slimy dog." "Give me twenty-five push-ups." "Get out of the sack, we're going for our 4:00 A.M. run." "Dig that latrine two feet deeper."

Lazy, overweight executives will get whipped into shape. They will learn to get up off their butts and work. Chronic abusers will be belittled and screamed at by a really mean drill sergeant until they're reduced to Jell-O. There will be some risks, of course. Muscle pulls will be the rule of the day. Frequent heart attacks should be expected. There will be the occasional guy who becomes permanently catatonic because he just can't take it. However, the survivors will be much improved. The weight will come off and the muscles and mind will trim up.

But, you say, "Aren't some managers already doing this kind of stuff?" My well thought out and articulate response is...Not even close! Outward Bound or those guys shooting paintballs at each other, is not what I have in mind. They are half-hearted three or four day efforts. They're just playing Boy

Scout: dressing in army fatigues, sleeping in tents, eating army rations and scaling forty-foot cliffs. They should get merit badges. Let's get serious. You can't break someone down in a weekend. Management boot camp should last a minimum of one hundred twenty days. Brainwash away all that bogus management nonsense...build the ideal executive from scratch.

Corporate Lunacy

Chapter 2 - Your Mission, Should You Choose to Accept It

Some strange life-forms inhabit the corporation.

Corporate Lunacy

3 WHO ARE THESE PEOPLE?

You'd better learn about all the animals in a corporation and their exceedingly strange habits before you take your seat in the menagerie. Who could have predicted that corporate evolution would have produced such types? The *scientific geeks*, strange little creatures with antennae and clammy skin, are surprising enough. But what about the *environmental specialists* aloft on the magic carpet of government mandated expenditure – they never needed to develop wings. And the *accountants* lurking beneath the computer printouts, babbling bookkeeping buzzwords. I'll also introduce you to the *lawyers*, shiny teeth all agleam. And those strutting *MBA's* in their fresh new peacock feathers. Marvel at the *consultants*, their lamprey-like mouths adapted for long-term engagement. Not to mention the company *psychologist* with his head up his tail searching for truth. Let's go visiting. But don't feed them peanuts; they may not understand.

GEEKS GALORE – Engineers, Programmers, Scientists

"Pure mathematics consists entirely of assertions to the effect that, if such and such a proposition is true of anything, then such and such another proposition is true of that thing. It is essential not to discuss whether the first proposition is really true, and not to mention what the anything is, of which it is supposed to be true."
Bertrand Russell (1872-1970)

Hold on to your pocket protectors. Here come the engineers, programmers and scientists...geeks! They breezed through college calculus, physics and the other technical stuff while you and I struggled. Each generation of geeks has become progressively smarter but stranger than the last.

Geeks are high-intelligence, terminally weird, compulsive problem-solvers that make the rest of us look retarded. Advances in science have created the opportunity for them to design even more things that none of the rest of us can understand. Take, for example, the computer, nuclear science, bio-genetics and artificial intelligence. I have no idea how any of these things works, do you?

Engineers, programmers and research scientists do not mix well with planners, accountants, marketers, production managers or general managers (or anyone else for that matter). They have a habit of designing things that no one else really wants simply to please themselves.

Corporate Lunacy

Left on their own, they will create something that works splendidly but is prohibitively expensive. The financial and operating people will then demand that the item be made – at ten percent of the cost. The result: American industry produces stuff that is often totally different from its original design. It may or may not work well, but it will be cheap.

Irving Smallwood, a research scientist, was a typical geek. Jeez, was he smart, but he had an annoying need to demonstrate his superior knowledge. He also had a compulsion for total honesty. You soon realized that you must never allow him to talk to customers or management. He particularly liked describing every potential fault in a given product. Irving tended to set these doubtlessly very interesting discussions in motion at the worst possible times, and he could never understand why veins would begin to pop out in the neck of Ed Markey, the Vice President of Sales.

Style didn't matter to Irving...his fetish was function. Fancy dresser? Hardly. Why the pocket protector? "Silly, wouldn't want ink (from the pen he forgot to put the top on) to leak all over my almond-colored rayon shirt."

That shirt went so well with the double-knit green polyester suit that he recently purchased from Kmart. Actually, he had recently purchased it in the late sixties. Why would he wear a black belt with that brown suit? Because it was his best belt and it held up his pants! White socks with his business suit? "They are 100 percent wool and absorb foot perspiration without harmful dyes."

Lester Brown was an engineer at a chemical company. He believed everything must be done to a certain standard. Remember that engineers are the ones who brought us ISO 9000!

In a future book, I will explore ISO 9000 in detail, if I can ever figure out what the hell it is. I do know it has something to do with generating huge piles of paper, documenting and labeling everything and essentially stopping production.

Lester would weigh a "quarter-pounder" hamburger to assure that it was exactly a quarter pound. Perhaps you told him he was being too picky? He would look at you in amazement: "What if that rocket nose cone was within about 1/1000 inch of tolerance, instead of exactly 1/1000 inch? Don't you understand that two plus two equals four; it doesn't equal some number between one and ten?"

Like most engineers, Lester had no concept of cost or even the function of money. Leading-edge design was all that mattered. For instance, he and his team were intent on using coal to produce electricity and steam in a major new plant they were designing. They wanted an alternative fuel to oil and natural gas, even though coal was not cost-effective. They designed an expensive, oversized and uncompetitive fluidized-bed system based on unproven technology.

Then there was George Savin, the computer programmer. George was always trying to convince you to let him build a database. He just knew you needed a database, but he had no idea why. His notion was that if you produced the data now, you could search for a reason later.

One day, George told you that your department's computer was not adequate to meet the growth needs of your company. He proposed two new computer solutions. One choice would cost $20,000 and the other $300,000. The expensive computer would do some high-tech stuff that only George could understand, but either would get the job done. Which one did George recommend? Do I have to tell you? The expensive one, of course. Why? Because it was state-of-the-art! The rest of you could suck wind for all he cared.

So, how can the intellect-challenged among us do our job in the face of the awesome but misplaced brainpower of the geeks?

1. **Do a value engineering study**. Put a brake on the state-of-the-art crazies with value engineering. Always look at price versus technology tradeoffs.

2. **Employ best practices**. Insist on a cost comparison of your project with similar projects designed by your competitors.

3. **Show more empathy and understanding**. Go hug a geek! It's worth a shot. Don't be disappointed in the

reaction, though. Love is an emotion unknown to geekdom because it isn't quantifiable.

4. **Do the job yourself.** Maybe the rest of us could go out and learn something about mechanics. Then again, I can't even program my VCR.

ACCOUNTANTS – The Bean Counters

"Sir, you are like a pin, but without either its head or its point."
Douglas William Jerrold (1803-57)

Ever wonder what happened to Ernie Gamble, that boring little twerp who sat next to you in high school math? He was always raising his hand to give the answer. He was a magnet for the school bullies. Remember when they "pantsed" him and then crammed him in his own gym locker? Well, guess what? Ernie grew up to become an accountant.

Today, Ernie is the type of person who blends into the walls of the institution. A visitor will rarely notice him. His office is always piled high with papers and manuals. Computer runs are everywhere – on his desk, the table, the chair and top of the filing cabinet. But Ernie wants the financial books to be as pristine as his office is messy.

Remember when he urged the departments to pay all their bills early so he could eliminate accruals on the year-end

financial statements?

Ernie just loves numbers. You'll hear him talk, with reverence, about budgeted net income in the fourth quarter of some future year as if it had already happened. He expresses rough estimates to five decimal places.

He would rather be precisely wrong than approximately correct...just so the numbers foot. And why do they use the word "foot" rather than, say, brain?

As a senior accountant, Ernie thrives on throwing cold water on good ideas. He will look at you like the in-bred bald guy in Deliverance who says, "You don't know nuthin, do ya?" "Don't you know you've got a real 13b problem here?"

Bud Hinken is a tax accountant. He is even more incomprehensible than Ernie is. Try the following to see how rapidly you doze off. I'm not making this up! "Excess net passive income cannot exceed the corporation's taxable income without regard to any net operating loss deduction (Code Sec. 172) and without regard to the special deductions allowed by Code Secs. 241-249, other than the amortization deduction for organizational expenditures of Code Sec. 248 (Code Sec. 1375 (b)(1)(B)."

Huh? The scary part is that Bud enjoyed reading this stuff, understood it and found it a helpful simplification.

Bud has made complexity an art form. He once worked on an easy little run-of-the-mill 401B-3 problem. He structured an offshore corporation as a partnership for U.S. tax purposes. Now, he simply wants to have a trust issue preferred stock treated as debt for tax purposes, so that 1099s can be issued instead of K-1s. Why yes, of course.

Accounting used to be simple. Everything was expressed in terms of historical cost – things that had actually happened. Then a group of accountants at the Financial Accounting Standards Board (a.k.a. The Institute of Immaculate Thought) decided to "accrue" for things that might happen in the future. They took plain old boring but understandable accounting and made it dynamic and incomprehensible.

Let's look at some of the words that accountants use in financial statements:

Corporate Lunacy

A. **Goodwill** – This is what companies get when they pay too much for an acquisition. "Goodwill" is the difference between what they paid and what the business was actually worth. I wonder, do you have "ill-will" when you get a bargain? Goodwill sounds good, doesn't it? You know, "Peace on Earth, goodwill to men." If it's so good, why is it a charge to income for the next 40 years?

B. **Credit** – In the non-financial world, credit means to bring honor upon. For example, "He's a credit to his father." But accountants credit an account, no kidding, to reduce it. When a company foolishly spends money on a new airplane, accountants credit cash and debit property (planes). Now, the debit part is a waste of resources, but they are enhancing (crediting) cash by spending it!

C. **Equity** – Ah ha! This must have to do with fairness: "He stands for truth and equity." Wrong again! Equity is all the profits the company has kept for itself. Some fairness!

D. **Fully Diluted Earnings** – Watered down...maybe it's just a flavor of true earnings? Wrong again! We are talking about pure, concentrated earnings after adjustments.

Chapter 3 - Who Are These People?

E. **Preferred Stock** – As opposed to unwanted stock? I prefer cash, thank you.

F. **Gross Profit** – Unseemly, as in disgusting, gross, usurious or odorous profit? Of course not; they mean "really big."

G. **Capital** – Major, important, primo, such as capital punishment or capital offense? Not on your life! They're referring to the money the business got by borrowing or selling stock.

H. **Cash and Cash Equivalents** – Hey, give me a break; either it is cash or it isn't!

Maybe accountants like Ernie and Bud create this confusion for job security. Maybe they know that a deluxe CD-ROM edition of *Quick Books* could replace them all. Or maybe they are just frustrated because they weren't obnoxious enough to become auditors.

Because you and I can't understand Ernie or Bud, has life become hopeless? Not at all! There are numerous support and group counseling resources available to help us cope. Take another Valium and relax...nobody else understands this stuff, either.

If an Ernie or a Bud confronts you, simply look him straight in the eye and say, "The statements are wrong and it's

Corporate Lunacy

up to you to correct them." If you are assertive, they will back down and ask, "What result did you have in mind?"

LAWYERS – Sharks and other Predators

"I would be loath to speak ill of any person who I do not know deserves it, but I am afraid he is an attorney."
Samuel Johnson (1709-84)

The sharkskin suit of the Corporate Attorney is testament to the close bond they share with their undersea relative, the shark. They possess a litigious skeletal structure; are aggressive carnivores; and will assault even members of their own species. Even the most seemingly docile will attack the defenseless. To a large extent they are scavengers, feeding on the weak or injured. They have an acute sense of smell, allowing them to detect even the minutest chance of a fee. When hunting in schools, they can incite one another into a feeding frenzy on a helpless victim.

Like sharks, there are considerable differences within the lawyer species. Some will quickly eat you alive, while others will

Chapter 3 - Who Are These People?

slowly suck you dry. Many are only dangerous when provoked, while others will attack at the hint of weakness. Some do little but sleep. Others are constantly moving, circling and thrashing.

Some of the more common varieties found in the world of corporate attorneys are:

The Great White Shark
(CRIMINAL DEFENSE ATTORNEY) *Criminalae Defensis.*

Rightly considered the most dangerous of the sharks, these predators exhibit great strength and terrify humans and low paid prosecuting attorneys with whom they come in contact. However, most authorities agree that their villainous reputation is undeserved (unless cameras are in the courtroom and big fees and book deals are a prospect).

This particular breed is not often found in the corporate world, although criminal behavior by top executives sometimes attracts them. Most corporate attorneys, in their secret moments, lust for the notoriety and wealth of the trial defense lawyer. They are the pop-rock stars of the profession.

The Tiger Shark
(TAKEOVER ATTORNEY) *Attilae the Huniformes.*

The suits with overstated stripes make recognition of this species simple. Colored shirts with white collars, cuff links and gaudy, tasteless ties mark the breed. Members will attack when they smell the fear of a panicky CEO afraid of losing his company.

Tiger sharks often swim in company with investment bankers, takeover artists and other corporate barracudas. They are known to feed with rapacious zeal in the name of releasing shareholder value.

The Puff Shark
(CORPORATE GENERAL COUNSEL) *Arrogantae Tediosiformes.*

This breed is a curious mutation that resulted from breeding a Blowfish with a Whale Shark. Normally small when judged by their own competence, they puff up to enormous size when inflated with their self-importance. This is especially true if the particular specimen is Harvard educated.

Feeding on insecure executives and other corporate flotsam, these sharks swim in circles so perfect that they never reach a conclusion. They are frequently found in the company of politicians and other high mucketymucks at Washington cocktail parties. Their boorish opinions are accompanied by strange Hrrrrrumph sounds.

The Hammerhead Shark
(LITIGATION SPECIALIST) *Callousae Insensitiviformes.*

Large flattened extensions of the head give these creatures the ability to track helpless prey. They can make sharp turns, particularly when needing to perform a defensive maneuver called CYA (cover your ass). They are totally fearless under most conditions. However, in the presence of a superior they become obsequious, groveling and servile.

Hammerheads are known to bring the full weight of the corporation to bear upon weak, unfortunate individuals. No lawsuit is too petty for them to engage in. They will unrelentingly hit their heads against obstacles such as principles and ethics and will attempt to mate with anything.

The Mako Shark
(CORPORATE SECRETARY) *Absurdae Policiformes.*

These unusual lawyers create policies out of their interpretation of what was said at a board meeting. None of the board would recognize the "board minutes" these creatures take. The origin of the term "Mako" is, "To Mako Mountain out of a molehill."

This species can be territorial and even ferocious if questioned. However, they will flee to the safety of obfuscation if pursued with facts. They are predominately found at seminars with their own kind. They feed on enormous reams of paper.

Cookie Cutter Shark
(CONTRACT ATTORNEY) *Bureaucratae Makeworkiformes.*

These creatures are noted for their symbiotic relationship with the word processor. They feed on plagiarism and are without original thought.

They drown their unsuspecting prey in a sea of stultifying verbiage. They eat and excrete from the same orifices. They cannot distinguish input from output. They negotiate from position to position on a wave of minutiae while avoiding the big picture.

Apparently, they breed like rabbits because they are quite numerous.

Reefer Shark
(ENVIRONMENTAL ATTORNEY) *Environmentae Dogoodiformes.*

These attorneys are distinguished by their save-the-world rhetoric. They will kill anything that doesn't agree with their message of peace, love and saving the environment. They are characterized by a large mouth and objectionable habits established in graduate school.

With a tendency to rush frantically in circles and make curious Beeeeeeemurrrrrr sounds, these sharks combine a lack of wisdom with a deficiency of understanding. Insufficiency of facts is not a hindrance to their zeal in finding a good scapegoat.

The Nurse Shark
(PATENT ATTORNEY) *Documentae Arcaniformes.*

Other legal professionals do not recognize these unfortunate creatures as real attorneys. They are slow, rather docile creatures, more a nuisance than a threat. They feed on academic and arcane literature.

It is unclear why they exist, because they are not known to procreate. Shy, they are not often seen except in the library.

The Remora

(PARALEGAL) *Faux Attornae Wanabeiformes.*

While these are not true attorneys, they superficially resemble bonafide lawyers. They swim attached to attorneys and feed on their scraps, but they are smaller and less pompous than their hosts.

Remoras scurry frantically at the behest of senior attorneys and do things no respectable (*sic*) lawyer would do. They make sounds like grunts. They have not passed the bar and spend most of their time buried in mountains of aged documents.

In general, lawyers have learned how to take the opposite side of every issue. They debate everything, find fault everywhere and can defend even the most untenable position. **To properly handle these creatures, do the following:**

1. **Treat them like the beasts they are.**
2. **Refer to them as non-team players.**
3. **Don't ask them what to do**...only how to do it.
4. **Never let them negotiate**; only allow them to commit agreed business deals to paper.
5. **Keep them busy standardizing contracts.**
6. **Suggest outplacing the whole department.**

ENVIRONMENTAL SPECIALISTS – That Stuff Could Kill Ya – Maybe!

"The sky is falling, the sky is falling."
Chicken Little (recently)

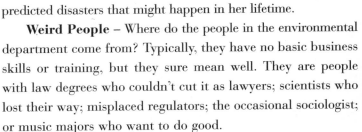

Environmental specialists are really weird dudes! They create problems rather than solve them. They make you worry, spend money and file reports, but you never know what they are trying to say because they won't give you a straight answer. They try to scare the hell out of you...about things that could happen two thousand years from now. Do you think you will care a whole lot by then? At least Cassandra predicted disasters that might happen in her lifetime.

Weird People – Where do the people in the environmental department come from? Typically, they have no basic business skills or training, but they sure mean well. They are people with law degrees who couldn't cut it as lawyers; scientists who lost their way; misplaced regulators; the occasional sociologist; or music majors who want to do good.

Weird Communications – Reinhardt Narren was the Manager of Environmental Protection at Acme Corporation.

He spoke Environmentaleeze, a weird bunch of acronyms that was incomprehensible to normal people. If you thought you knew what Narren was saying, he hadn't made himself clear. He quoted from huge books about DNAPL (dense non-aqueous phase liquid) and LNAPL (light non-aqueous phase liquid). George Welbly (Acme's CEO) knew that there must be something in those big words to be concerned about, but he had no idea what it was.

Let's listen in on a typical discussion between Welbly and Reinhardt Narren:

Welbly: "Do we have a problem?"

Narren: "We may! We have checked the pond and found twenty ppb of PCB."

Welbly: "Twenty ppb doesn't sound like a lot to me. Is that bad?"

Narren: "Well, it could be. We have simulated circumstances where it is."

Welbly: "Does it violate any laws?"

Narren: "Well, maybe, depending on whether we have permits."

Welbly: "Permits for what?"

Narren: "For releasing PCB."

Welbly: "Oh, it's okay if we have a permit?"

Narren: "Well, it may or may not be under some conditions."

Corporate Lunacy

Welbly:	"Did we cause this problem?"
Narren:	"Well, clearly we may have, but then again we may not. We've got to measure the migration of the plume."
Welbly:	"If we didn't cause it, who did?"
Narren:	"It could have come from an adjacent property. On the other hand, it might have occurred naturally."
Welbly:	"Well, then, what should we do?"
Narren:	"We need a study to understand the complex geological issues."
Welbly:	"By the way, what is PCB?"
Narren:	"It is blah, blah, blah, blah, blah, blah...but we still need a study."

All environmental discussions end this way. The expert will say, "We need a study!"

Weird Studies – So Welbly commissioned a $20,000 study to determine what was really there, and what did Narren find? He found that there may or may not be a problem. Acme had only done a Phase One study! They scanned a few records and walked around looking for distressed vegetation (they could have found that on my lawn). A Phase Two study was needed. Welbly asked, "Will Phase Two, at $300,000, answer the problem?" Narren answered unequivocally, "It may or may not. We need to test!"

Weird Science – Narren was an alarmist, talking doomsday without any real facts. Acme's PCB problem was related to an aquifer and a geological fault that could put the stuff in someone's drinking water! If unchecked, it would either pollute Lake Erie, or New Orleans, possibly as soon as 200 years from now. Huh? Can't we narrow it down a bit? Exasperated, Welbly said, "Aren't we talking about twenty ppb in over 200 years, after it's been diluted to an undetectable level?" Narren looked at him like he was Adolph Hitler! Condescendingly, he replied, "If everyone took that attitude, we would all be standing waste-deep in PCBs right now."

Weird Remedies – We have to remediate! This means that Acme will have to use some technology that no one knows for sure will work in order to not necessarily cure a problem that they are not sure is a problem at all.

Note that some environmental "remedies" only make things worse. For example, take a building that has PACM (Presumed Asbestos Containing Materials). What can the environmentalists do? They can take the stuff out, of course, releasing once safely confined asbestos particles into the air where they can hurt someone. Remember, these materials were only presumed to contain asbestos in the first place.

Weird Technology – It was found that Acme had 0.000889 ppb of DCP in the ground under its headquarters. If this property ever became a day care center, the kids might dig it up. What to do? What to do? Narren thought the stuff might evaporate, if they could just spray it into the air! Of course, Acme would need a permit to do so at a cost of $10,000.

To get it out of the ground (where it really threatens nobody) Acme must pump a bunch of other stuff in. This other stuff would push out the first stuff, spraying it into the air. (Don't you love this technical talk?) According to Narren, this would cause all that first stuff to go away. I always thought that you could not destroy or create matter. So where did all the DCP go?

Narren said there's some bad stuff in the soil. Acme must therefore take out all of the earth in a 200x200x30ft. area and replace it with good dirt from somewhere else. (Sounds like the army). They must then take the bad soil someplace where it can be concentrated with other sludge. Welbly wondered, "Do they hire someone to watch the bad dirt until it goes away?"

Big Bucks – As crazy (and as costly) as this stuff is, nothing ever really gets cleaned up. A whole new industry has arisen, though, which has grown to $150 billion in revenues from only $10 billion twenty-five years ago.

The environment is dirtier than ever, but the hazardous waste management, remediation, consulting, instrument monitoring, resource recovery, analytical services and government agencies are doing just fine, thank you!

Chapter 3 - Who Are These People?

Mathematically, it looks like this:

WP+WS+WT+BG = BB where:
WP = weird people
WS = weird science
WT = weird technology
BG = big government
BB = big bucks

Well, let's explore what to do with these frustrating people.

1. **Don't ever hire an internal Environmental Department**. But if one already exists:
2. **Hire your own consultant** (who speaks their language) to dispute whatever they say.
3. **Put them in charge of a taskforce** to compare your company's environmental issues and practices to your competitor's.
4. **Send them away to seminars**. On second thought, maybe global warming is the result of all the hot air generated at these seminars.

Corporate Lunacy

INFURIATING MBAs.

"He was like a cock who thought the sun had risen to hear him crow."
George Eliot (1819-80)

MBAs...Ptuii! The obnoxious little weasels want to run your company, but their analysis is superficial and their prescriptions are ill-conceived. They are typically egocentric, reality-challenged, immature and overpaid.

The worst of the lot come from the "Top Ten" business schools, as defined by Business Week and other surveys. Something happened when those kids inhaled the rarefied air

Send in the President, I need to see him now.

Chapter 3 - Who Are These People?

at Harvard, Wharton, Virginia, Northwestern, or Stanford. But corporations usually get the bottom half of the MBA barrel. All of Harvard's Baker Scholars go to the consulting firms.

The curriculum of MBA schools is oriented toward getting high-paying jobs, not academic excellence. Instructors who never worked in a business teach teamwork, leadership, ethics and globalization. Other courses include writing resumes, interviewing, restaurant etiquette, scheduling travel and sucking up to management. Classes in accounting, statistics, marketing, personnel and logistics are now de-emphasized.

In many ways Mel looked like a typical MBA. He was twenty-four years old and had a total of three years of business experience as a junior accountant at a small firm. But Mel was special — a graduate of Harvard. He had gained a superficial understanding of business strategy by doing a Case Study, where he was assigned to a team of five students that solved all the problems of General Motors and AT&T in a semester. Golly...They even wrote a definitive twenty-seven page paper and proclaimed themselves to be marvelously effective after "bonding" at an Outward Bound weekend in the Poconos.

Well, Acme Corporation thought they had a real gem when they hired Mel. He received a salary of $85,000 a year plus a signing bonus of $20,000. But they should have seen the danger signs. Mel said he needed to take three months off before he joined the company to travel through Europe. After all, he needed to regenerate his motor because graduate school had been so exhausting.

Corporate Lunacy

Mel was assigned to the Finance Department. It was here that his lack of useful skills and poor business judgment surfaced. He was supposed to assure the timely payment of interest on the company's debt. His system consisted of Post-it notes stuck around his desk. Because of Mel, the company was periodically in default. Luckily, Acme had a good relationship with its bankers.

Mel certainly knew how to run up the expenses, though. As he became acquainted with the various consultants who worked with the company, Mel would call them for assistance. He always acted as if Stubblefield (the Senior Executive Vice President of Finance) had asked him to call.

The consultants were happy to oblige Mel because they could run the clock and increase their billings to the company. Mel calling...Ka-ching! Accounting bills rose, actuaries' bills increased and lawyers' fees skyrocketed. At first no one realized what was happening. Then, one by one the departments began asking about the increases. The same answer kept coming up: Mel.

Any project assigned to Mel turned into a disaster, starting with that competitive analysis. Mel could find no company that was exactly like Acme, so he concluded the company really had no competitors. Mostly, though, Mel spent his time running an office football pool. If he wasn't doing that, he was on the phone making long distance calls to his bookie or his college buddies.

Mel treated secretaries with disdain, even causing one to quit. Mel was always scheduling meetings with senior management. The last straw was when he scheduled a meeting to help Welbly (the CEO) rethink his strategy. The normally calm Welbly screamed, "Fire that little twerp!"

However, by the time HR had its ducks in a row, Mel had turned in his resignation.

It seems that Acme was just another notch on Mel's resume. He landed a big job, with a forty percent increase in salary, at one of those competitors Mel swore the company didn't have.

Then there was Steve, another MBA who wound up in corporate finance. He drooled at the thought of issuing MIPS, QUIPS, MIITS, TIGERS and Equity Linked Notes. It carbonated his hormones to do swaps, options, collars, forwards, yield curve plays and dynamic hedges.

He spent seventy-two hours without sleep working with lawyers, bankers and the accountants on a finance deal. When the deal was done, he was smelly but proud. The investment banker pocketed a fee of about $5 million. Steve got an acrylic cube (worth $1.47) to put on his desk.

Buffy believed she had special insights into the market from her vantage point in Akron, Ohio. She had never taken more than a beginning course in economics, but she would wax eloquently on the interest rate environment: "I think rates will rise this next year by 100 basis points and there will be a down-tick in the up-trend by year-end." She would pontificate and ruminate endlessly about Federal Reserve policy, but her track record was worse than a three-legged racehorse's.

Drew's resume was representative of all MBAs, filled with

hyperbole. His experience sounded impressive even though his previous positions were as a claims clerk and a Taco Bell counter boy. That's why he went back to school – to get a meaningful job and make more money. Do you think he would have bothered if his previous jobs were as swell as his resume portrayed? "Assisted in formulating strategic development recommendations" simply meant he typed papers.

The table below provides some assistance to help you translate the overblown resumes of guys like Drew:

BUZZWORD	WHAT IT REALLY MEANS
Responsible for	Was a scapegoat for a disaster and fired
Developed recommendations	Made no decisions of own
Facilitated	Got airline tickets for executives
Produced reports	Crunched numbers mindlessly
Participated in	Was present in room, but not allowed to speak
Created reports	Took papers to the copier
Performed due-diligence	Grubbed numbers
Supervised staff	Was allowed to observe people in action
Organized	Put tabs in binder for presentation

All MBA resumes try to portray a well-rounded individual. For example, "I enjoy politics, travel, movies, sports and discourses with people from varied backgrounds." Have you ever seen one that says, "I am a misanthrope and spend most of my time alone with Nintendo, watching the soaps and sloshing down beer?"

What a bunch! Steve's resume said he worked on Wall Street, but he really only delivered the mail at Merrill Lynch. Drew prepared a report lambasting the marketing division and then went off to "help" logistics management. Buffy, without authorization, bought leveraged foreign currency derivatives and cost the company $23 million. Heather, at twenty-three years of age, thought she could tell Webster, the VP of Production (who had thirty-six years of experience), that he didn't know what he was doing. And of course there was Mel! What can you say about Mel?

Luckily, the half-life of an MBA is short. They will probably leave for greener pastures before they even learn their job. Only about one out of twenty will stay as long as three years.

COMPANY PSYCHOLOGISTS – Palmreaders

"A psychiatrist is a man who goes to the Follies-Bergere and looks at the audience."
Bishop Mervyn Stockwood (b. 1913)

Wow! Great news, but why are you also troubled? "We're

Corporate Lunacy

thinking of putting you on the fast track," said your boss, Leland Oberstar. "I want you to schedule an appointment with Dr. Tolpel. He interviews all candidates for upper-middle management positions." (Eric Tolpel was a management psychologist who had a consulting relationship with the company.)

You were enthused about the promotional possibility, but concerned about the psychologist. You wondered, "What if they are gathering ammunition to can my butt?" Steady now…don't let the paranoia take hold. Just schedule the appointment.

So who is this guy Tolpel? He isn't a licensed psychiatrist, but he doesn't correct people who call him Doctor. His highest degree is a master's in psychology. He secretly feels that he is less competent than a psychiatrist, and his feelings of inferiority are warranted.

Tolpel, a misplaced sociologist, intuitively hates the type of individual that would make a good manager. He neither understands nor likes business. He would be a miserable manager himself. Tolpel is essentially a palmreader with an advanced degree. Palmreaders, however, will at least tell you what they observe. Tolpel will tell everyone but you.

What will the interview be like? Tolpel has scheduled two hours to determine if you are fit for upper-middle management. First, he will interrogate you for about an hour. What's he hiding behind that beard and mustache? He'll ask questions but will give you no feedback. What's he thinking when he nods knowingly?

Then he will give you a Rorschach test and a 45-question multiple-choice intelligence test. From this brief glimpse of your life, Tolpel will reach conclusions that affect the rest of your career. You will never see the results, but you can be sure the company relies on this stuff.

How should you act? To have a successful interview, your adult ego-state must connect with Tolpel's adult ego-state. Don't allow your parent ego-state to clash with his child ego-state or he will view you as a tyrant. Don't let his parent ego-state engage your child ego-state or he will think you lack leadership. Isn't this fun? Get him to talk about his feelings. Empathize! Both give and occasionally ask for feedback. For goodness sake, don't tell him you think he is pathetic!

He's looking for buzzwords to put in a report, so give him a few. You want "gets things done" as well as "sensitive to others' needs" to appear in his report. Show him that you are confident but humble by taking one of your strengths and casting it as a weakness. For example, say, "My desire to make the company the best it can be sometimes causes me to be impatient with those who don't have my unbelievable level of commitment."

Corporate Lunacy

You want him to think you have the empathy of Mother Theresa; that you could convince armies to lay down their arms and convert them into farm equipment; and that your leadership abilities rival those of Gandhi, Churchill, or Clinton? Oops! Must be a typo. Oh well...hopefully he just won't sabotage your career.

What will he produce? First, Tolpel fills out a worksheet for a number of character traits. Then he plugs the data into a word processing program. This creates a *Skills* and *Personality Profile* that sounds as if it was written about you. It will be put into your personnel file where it will sit like a time bomb.

The *Profile* purports to be a thoughtful, deep analysis of your strengths and weaknesses. However, it's guaranteed to be a mishmash of broad-brush nonsense. It will be accessible to senior management and also to the busybodies in HR, who will probably share it with their friends.

Tolpel prepares his report using WIMPI characteristics: Work-habits, Intelligence, Management, Personality and Interpersonal relations. Each characteristic has eight to ten elements; so ostensibly, the report covers forty to fifty of your characteristics. About three or four pages of high-class stuff will be written about you. A summary and conclusions will restate what was previously written.

The report will be of about the same quality as the analysis of a psychic advisor. Isn't it swell that, "You are determined, aggressive, caring and desirable." His report is to psychiatric analysis what paint-by-numbers is to serious art.

Chapter 3 - Who Are These People?

Let's look at part of the interpersonal relations section of Tolpel's worksheet:

Interpersonal Relations

I. Awareness of others' opinions (choose one).

   A. Has an awareness of others' feelings.

   B. Uses others' ideas if they will be useful.

   C. Will use others' ideas if they agree with his own.

   D. Shows disdain for the ideas of others.

II. Conflict management (choose one).

   A. Is adept at conflict management.

   B. Will attempt to sway others to own opinion by logic.

   C. Will attempt to force conclusions by resorting to fear tactics.

   D. Ignores controversy and writes reports the way he wants them.

III. First Impressions (choose one).

   A. The first impression is that of a leader.

   B. Depending on the situation, can be either charming or appear cold and aloof.

   C. Creates an impression that he is tentative about his value.

   D. Appears lost in the clouds.

Corporate Lunacy

If Tolpel had marked down B, B and D from the above, this section of the report would read:

This is an individual who tends to exhibit his awareness of others' opinions by using others' ideas if they can be useful. In managing conflict, he will attempt to sway others to his own opinions by logic. He has redeeming qualities, but one's first impression is that he appears lost in the clouds.

What will they do with the report? In spite of the fact that this is all drivel, the report will be in your personnel file forever. It is frightening that some managers will even think it is useful.

So, the darned thing is important and you should make Tolpel your friend and establish a bond by:

1. **Giving him the key words** that he can use to fill out his worksheet.
2. **Helping him write his subsequent report.**
3. **Not laughing** at his lack of standing among his peers.
4. **Suggesting** that if you ever become the boss, you will double his retainer. I can guarantee this will get you the best damn *Skills* and *Personality Profile* ever.

CONSULTANTS – Leaches and Parasites

"Man is the only animal that can remain on friendly terms with the victims he intends to eat until he eats them."
Samuel Butler (1835-1902)

Consultants will latch onto a company like your brother-in-law to your wallet. Like leaches and parasites, once they are engaged, you can't get rid of them. Companies hire consulting firms based on the fast talk and reputation of their senior partners. However, companies rarely see a partner after they sign up. Instead, they get an army of wet-behind-the-ears associates. Then about once a month, the senior partner will spend a couple of hours of face-time with the CEO, delivering theater tickets, trips to Bermuda, fancy dinners, elaborate Christmas gifts, sports tickets and the best wines. The consulting firm charges the cost of these bribes back to the company with a markup.

Consultants spout buzzwords to make it sound as if they understand your company. If your company is centralized, they will recommend decentralization. If your company is decentralized, they will point to a lack of control and the need to centralize. Have you ever heard of a consultant saying, "Everything looks swell to me?"

Only one measure of success is meaningful to the consultant – billable hours. You know how a tailor looks at you, trying to guess whether you are a size 38 or a size 40 regular? And morticians – they're always trying to size you up, too. Well, consultants do the same thing, but what do they see when they look at you? Billable hours, that's what.

Corporate executives who were fired because they were useless or had stupid ideas become senior consultants. The guilt-ridden firm that fired them often hires them again as a consultant, at more than their former salary. Those goofy ideas that no one would listen to before suddenly become corporate action plans because they're now recommended by a consultant.

Senior consultants bill out at up to $700 an hour, according to the 1996 survey of consulting fees conducted by the Kennedy Research Group. How hard do they work for this kind of money? Let's put it this way: have you ever met a senior consultant who wasn't a better golfer than you are?

Junior consultants are usually new MBAs who have no business experience or judgment. Basically, they don't know squat, except the latest academic buzzwords and theories, but they think they have all the answers. The sum total of their knowledge comes from business courses taught by professors who never worked for a real company. Junior consultants will work incredibly long hours grubbing data and will treat your staff like pond scum. These inept but energetic fellows bill out at $100 an hour.

George Welbly, Acme's CEO, bragged that he was once a consultant for a big-name consulting firm. In fact, the consulting firm he worked for had an "up or out" policy, and Welbly couldn't cut it. So, as with other rejects, the firm found him a senior management job in the corporate world.

Welbly always hired a "name firm" like Booz Allen, McKinsey (his former employer), Boston Consulting Group, Bain or Anderson Consulting Group in order to give credence to the otherwise superficial nonsense the consultants produced. But no matter who the company hired, Acme got nothing more than the most recent panacea or fad. In one case, Acme was given a report that was created for another company.

A typical project team for an Acme consulting engagement consisted of a partner, four project managers, sixteen consultants and sixteen associates. It cost Acme about $250,000 a month. These teams always produced large reports, which essentially told Welbly what he wanted to hear. Then the consultants would ask for more money, suggest the need for further study and perhaps a long-term contract.

Look back in history at how consultants have led their hosts to doom:

CONSULTANTS IN HISTORY

1. The serpent advised Adam that it was all right to bite the apple.
2. Delilah advised Samson that he would look better if he got a ninety's haircut.
3. A consultant advised the Trojans that a horse would be a swell thing to have at their Greek Week fraternity rush party.
4. Thomas More advised Henry VIII that he shouldn't keep marrying those women.
5. A consultant advised George I that a stamp tax wouldn't tick off the Colonies.
6. A consultant advised Napoleon that Waterloo would be a neat place for a fight.
7. Rasputin advised Alexandria that the Bolsheviks shouldn't be feared because they didn't have a good strategic plan.
8. Michael Milken advised Drexel Burnham that junk bonds meant big bucks.
9. An army of consultants advised, advised and advised AT&T, to the tune of about half a billion dollars.
10. Figgie Corp. hired consultants to cure the problems caused by other consultants.

Many management books give the following advice about dealing with consultants:

A. **Fire the consultants** and take back your company.

B. **Know very specifically what you want** before you hire a consultant.

C. **Demand the firm's best** – don't pay for partners and receive grunts.

D. **Don't give up the control** of your company to the consultants.

E. **Beware of long-term consulting engagements.**

Well, you can forget all this advice. It's directed at the .00001 percent of the people that are CEOs. The boss will decide how to handle the consultants and the rest of you can pound salt.

Corporate Lunacy

Chapter 3 - Who Are These People?

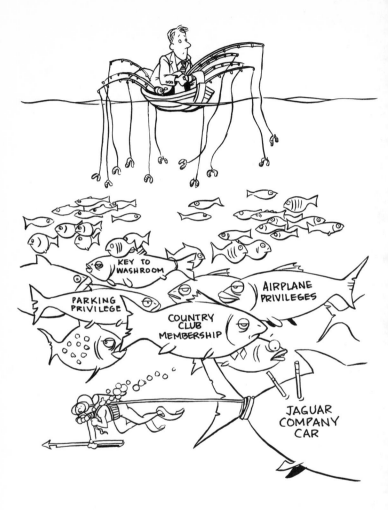

Ralph couldn't seem to land any "big fish"

Corporate Lunacy

4 GETTING YOUR SHARE

It certainly wouldn't be fair not to get your share...and who knows better than you what that share might be. In the modern corporation, you have the opportunity to draw your compensation from many wells. Don't be shy; many a person with an even greater thirst has been there before you. While the corporation is sucking out the last remnants of your brain (and perhaps your spinal cord with it), you might as well pad things out, get the greenbacks, pump up the frequent flyer miles, pamper yourself with perks and let the good times roll. Odds are you're earning it.

THE ART OF EXPENSE CONTROL – Consider it a Raise

"Grow your tree of falsehood from a small grain of truth."
Ceslaw Milosav (b. 1911)

Corporations are losing the war on employee business expenses. It isn't even a close battle. Workers are tenacious in their efforts to overcome expense controls. The more rules there are, the more the creative juices of petty larceny flow.

Some schemes amount to no more than burying the cost of candy for the office candy dish in an expense report. In contrast, relocation of managers is an opportunity for big-time expense padding. I pay special tribute here to the particularly ingenious efforts of some individuals to build airline frequent flier miles.

I. FREQUENT FLIER MILES ARE FABULOUS.

One of the most important developments in the war on business expenses was the advent of airline frequent flier programs. Many companies seeing the huge values building in their employees' frequent flier accounts attempted to gain control of these mileage balances for themselves. The employee riots that followed made the anti-war riots of the 1970s look like love-ins.

Companies learned that these accounts are a basic employee right and not to be taken lightly. Doesn't it follow that workers should assert their right by acquiring as many miles as possible?

Corporate Lunacy

Let's review some of the more basic techniques to build miles in your account:

A. **Add legs to a trip.** Is there any rule that says business travelers must fly by the most direct route? Flying from Cleveland to Santa Fe by way of Pittsburgh, Newark, Dallas and Houston gives you a lot more miles than a direct flight. It also invariably costs more...but you're not paying the freight.

B. **Pay full-fare coach.** Many of you probably think no one pays full-fare. Well, you're just plain wrong! One of the benefits of paying full-fare coach is that you can often get double the miles. Why book that saver-fare which requires fourteen days advance purchase? The reward for a last minute ticket is more mileage credit.

C. **Take advantage of promotions.** Spend some time reading the newest promotional deals to see how you can acquire more miles. If an airline is trying to build traffic on its route from Dallas to Atlanta, it will often give bonus miles. Why not make sure that this flight is included as one leg of your trip?

D. **Fly one airline preferentially.** It's a bummer having only a few miles with a lot of different airlines. What kind of a prize can you get for 4,938 miles? You need to focus your efforts on one airline, even if its fares are higher. Pay attention now…you're not the one paying for the ticket. Then, when you get that well-deserved bronze, silver or gold elite frequent flier card, you'll be able to enjoy free upgrades and bonus miles, too.

E. **Frequently fly those rental cars and hotels.** Most programs give you 500 frequent flier miles when you rent a car or check into a specific hotel. Therefore, don't rent a car for an entire week. Instead, turn in the car every day and then rent it again. You'll get 500 miles each time. For one week, you're talking 3,500 miles instead of 500. The same thing is true for hotels. Check out every day and then check right back in. Sound like a lot of work? Well, what are you willing to do to get that St. Martin vacation a few months sooner?

II. THE ADVANTAGES OF PAYING FULL-FARE COACH.

To save money, the corporation makes you fly coach. Do you like traveling in a cattle-car with four and a half inches of legroom, eating unidentifiable meat on a hard roll for dinner? Not to worry! The airlines often reward those people who are thoughtful enough to pay top dollar for their seats in coach.

For example, you might fly full-fare roundtrip coach to Seattle for $1,100 on Northwest. Luckily, there happens to be a promotion going that will automatically upgrade full-fare coach passengers to first class. You get a big seat, good food and all the free booze you can drink.

Now isn't that better than those little bitsy coach seats on Continental or U.S. Air at an advance discount fare of $400? Isn't your comfort worth the small amount someone else pays for it?

Another option forces you to make a tradeoff – your comfort for cold, hard cash. Here's how it works: Use your own credit card to book the lowest price super-saver fare. Next, buy that full fare ticket and then get a refund by turning the flight coupons back to the airline. Now you have a full-fare receipt for your expense records. You pocket the difference.

Is the complexity of this hurting your head? You think that this is like cheating? Silly you! Didn't you earn the money by flying at a lower priced fare? Would the company have paid the higher fare if it didn't want to?

Why are you so concerned about all those auditors hovering outside your door? A minor note: This scheme has resulted in the exchange of pinstripes for prison stripes on a few occasions.

III. WHAT'S SO BAD ABOUT THE CROWDED SKIES?

Flying the airlines that always overbook is a great way to make money and gain free travel. You can be the one who gives up your seat to some Type A guy who actually wants to get where he's going. You can get bumped and make a quick $200 or receive a discount certificate for your personal use. With practice and a wise selection of airlines, you should expect to be bumped at least half of the time.

Oh, I almost forgot — you should arrange your personal vacation around business trips. Take the wife along.

IV. MEALS ARE MARVELOUS.

There are some swell chances to earn extra money while dining on company funds. Ever notice how many $29.95 dinners there are on expense accounts when the meal allowance is $30? And haven't you always wanted a set of those neat heavy steak knives from Morton's? You can have them. Just add them to your bill one at a time. Just 8 dinners @ $12 a pop and you can have a complete set. Take that ashtray and salt and pepper set out of your pocket...stealing is wrong. Just say, "Add it to the bill."

V. TAXIS ARE TERRIFIC.

Some really keen scams are connected with cabs. How many people really pay that $45 cab fare from O'Hare to downtown Chicago that shows up on their expense account? The rapid transit at $3.50 is not a bad ride. Frankly, at rush hour it's a lot faster than the bumper-to-bumper freeways. How many people have ever tipped that belligerent cabby? It is always on their expense report, however. If you need some receipts, take a cab for a couple of blocks downtown. Cabbies are too lazy to fill out receipts themselves so they'll give you blanks. For a couple of bucks they'll give you some extras. What's wrong with sharing a cab and charging full fare? Isn't it marvelous what you can do when you get really creative?

Corporate Lunacy

VI. HOTEL EXPENSES CAN ADD UP.

It kind of ticks off those bellhops when you carry your own bag. However, if you use them it's almost impossible to get rid of them without a tip. The expense report rule here is, "Tip a dime and charge a dollar."

The valet is a special opportunity. I know a guy who probably never paid a laundry bill in his life. I think he saved up his dirty clothes and then took them on his business trips. You should have seen his valet bills.

VII. EXCHANGE RATE ECSTASY.

Foreign travel is fun because it involves other currencies. Complexity creates opportunity. Have you ever found an accountant who understands foreign exchange?

Charging on your personal American Express card assures you get the best exchange rates. You can pay for your hotel at this low exchange rate and then charge the company at the highest rates printed in the newspaper. All your other expenses qualify as well...use your imagination.

VIII. OPPORTUNITIES AT THE OFFICE.

Do you know how much you can cut your home phone bills if you make long-distance calls from the office? Now if you could only get the company to pay your teenagers' phone bills, you could probably get out of debt.

Take home office supplies for fun and profit and examine the possibilities for charging the company for your home

115

computer supplies. Modems, telephone cords and new batteries are a start. Almost unlimited possibilities exist for computer software. However, think twice about trying to get the company to pay for that new Power Rangers game.

Get to know the folks in marketing. They always have extra sports jackets, golf balls, shirts, etc. from their last meeting. Take advantage of the opportunity to build your wardrobe for free.

IX. MOVING EXPENSE MADNESS.

What if the company wants you to relocate? Now here's the place to cash in big. One guy (I swear this is true) moved 500 pounds of patio bricks, mulch and a side of beef he had just purchased – at the company's expense, of course.

Moves across national boundaries offer the maximum potential for monetary gain. Bill your expenses at the highest exchange rate in a month and pay them at the lowest. Always plead that it is more expensive to live where you are going than where you came from, and make sure you get an allowance for this difference.

Put your home up for sale at a ridiculously high price. Who knows, someone may pay it. If not, get a friendly appraisal for maximum benefit when the relocation company buys it. The relocation company isn't laying out its own money, so what the heck does it care?

X. WHAT ABOUT THE EXECUTIVES?

All the stuff we've discussed so far is really just chump

Corporate Lunacy

change. Committed executives, however, can spend some serious money (never their own). Forget about schemes to upgrade to first class; they're already there. Frequent flier miles? First class gets you double. That gold elite flier card helps a lot, too. Often, the company jet is available to ease the strain of travel. That fashion trip to Paris...it was business. Just happened to coincide with that important company meeting.

But, some executives are more concerned about money than comfort. Those with Spartan tastes can turn in their first class tickets, fly coach and pocket the difference. Comfort has a price, after all. These guys merely take their comfort in cash.

A night at the theatre, ballet or the symphony can be charged to the company. That trip to The Superbowl, The Master's at Augusta,...personal expense? Guess again! Fishing in Alaska – that was business development. Golf in Scotland at all the famous courses – customer cultivation. Of course that much fine wine was needed for the company function. A good executive simply puts the excess in his personal cellar for safekeeping.

Do you get the picture? While the executives live the good life, the rest of you lightly pad expense reports, make long distance calls at the office, grub for frequent flier miles and take home a few ball-point pens. If you're lucky, the company will be around long enough to give you a gold watch when you retire – or a golden handshake when you're downsized.

Chapter 4 - Getting Your Share

PERFORMANCE APPRAISAL – This is For Your Own Good.

"No one wants advice – only corroboration."
John Steinbeck (1902-68)

It's time for your performance appraisal and your boss, Oberstar, wants to give you a whole bunch of free advice. He says, "I want to help you be a self-actualized, fully functioning manager. I want to provide the guidance necessary for you to develop to the maximum of your potential. Let's review all of your strengths and weaknesses and then set out a development plan for

Corporate Lunacy

continuous improvement." Isn't that swell? Oberstar must really care! Hellllloooo...Wake up Van Winkle! Performance appraisals came from the mind of a deranged and sadistic human resources (HR) director. The guy was trained in interrogation at the Harvard Law School. The process is designed to make you feel like a specimen in a jar. Appraisals masquerade as personal improvement programs, but they also allow the company to build a CYA file on you. This file will provide legal support for the company when it terminates you.

Performance reviews can be terribly demotivating, resulting in feelings of failure and unhappiness. Even management doesn't always enjoy them. Leland Oberstar, for example, hates the performance appraisal process because he has to fill out a bunch of forms. Furthermore, there may be an argument...and he hates arguments. Take the last appraisal he did of Bud Hinken, the tax accountant:

Oberstar: "I've graded you as solidly in the good category."

Hinken: "I should be rated outstanding or at a minimum superior. Ernie Gamble was rated superior, and I am much better than he is."

Oberstar: "Ernie works harder than you do."

Hinken: "Ernie's just a brown nose."

Oberstar: "You don't show a high level of commitment."

Hinken: "I do so!"

Oberstar: "You do not."

Hinken:	"Do so."
Oberstar:	"Do not."
Hinken:	"Give me a for instance."
Oberstar:	"Well, you don't get to work on time."
Hinken:	"I always do."
Oberstar:	"What about last Tuesday."
Hinken:	"My mother was sick, my car broke down, my alarm didn't work and I had to stop at the pharmacy. You don't trust me."
Oberstar:	"Well uhh…how can we proceed from here?"
Hinken:	"If you grade me superior, I promise to work harder."
Oberstar:	"Well, if you promise, I guess we are moving in the right direction."

Oberstar left this confrontation with a gigantic headache. Bud Hinken walked away pissed off at Oberstar for rating him initially as merely good. He felt even more antagonistic because Oberstar changed the rating after he complained.

Oberstar will postpone Bud's next performance appraisal for as long as possible. He will either let Bud fill out his own evaluation or mark this mediocre complainer as outstanding and let it go at that.

Management gurus say to mix in positive feedback (a spoon full of sugar) with "suggestions for improvement." They think this will cause employees like Bud to accept criticism. The "experts" also say that conversations about compensation should be separated from conversations about performance.

Everyone is expected to pretend that this review won't have a bearing on money. Who are they kidding? Hinken knew that his rating directly affected his next merit increase – four percent if he's rated good, six percent if he's rated superior, a promotion if he's outstanding.

The experts tell managers not to dwell on the past...rather, look to the future. That's great! Everyone can visualize doing well in the future...the future hasn't happened yet. Wouldn't you opt to be judged by what you are going to do, rather than by what you have actually done?

These once-a-year performance appraisals rarely produce desirable results. So, what do the management gurus recommend now? You've got it! They want continuous appraisals.

They want to constantly examine you...like a monkey picking fleas.

How can you survive such constant corporate scrutiny?

1. **Practice your body language.** Set jaw, cross arms, stare daggers – make sure the boss knows you're not receptive to criticism.
2. **Insist on a superior rating.**
3. **Dispute any sign of a problem.**
4. **Write a counter-point for every point** your appraiser makes. Insist it go in your file. This will be useful in your future lawsuit.

SALARY AND COMPENSATION – Filthy Lucre

"Corporation. An ingenious device for obtaining individual profit without individual responsibility."
Ambrose Bierce (1842-1914)

How do corporations determine the salaries of their employees? Consulting firms make megabucks advising corporations on compensation matters. They specialize in making the simple complex. However, after conducting a major and expensive study, virtually any management compensation consultant will produce the same result.

You can pay the consultants millions, or you can buy a compensation manual for about seventy-five bucks, and do the job yourself.

All of the consultants' compensation systems really boil down to a couple of basic rules: No matter what your level in the organization, **Rule One:** Your salary will be approximately two-thirds higher than the salary of the level below you. **Rule Two:** Your total compensation will be approximately double that of the level below you. The word "approximately" allows the consultants to conceal the greed-based simplicity of salary administration.

The following table for the Acme Corporation shows how the salary rule works:

ACME SALARY STRUCTURE

POSITION	SALARY	INCREASE OVER PREVIOUS LEVEL
Clerk, secretary	$18,000	N/A (not appreciated)
Supervisor	$28,000	2/3
Manager	$46,000	2/3
Assistant V.P.	$78,000	2/3
Vice President	$130,000	2/3
Senior V.P.	$215,000	2/3
Executive V.P.	$360,000	2/3
President	$600,000	2/3
Chairman	$1,000,000	2/3

Now, wasn't that simple enough for even a government employee to understand? Many HR people will try to confuse you by renaming these positions. Consultants will add a bunch of sub-levels. Don't be fooled! People at each level (whatever it's called) will get two-thirds more than people at the next lower level. Everything works smoothly. The Sr. VP's salary is thirteen times the clerk's, the Exec. VP's is thirteen times the supervisor's, the President's is thirteen times the manager's, and the Chairman's is thirteen times the Assistant VP's salary.

Really has a simple symmetry, doesn't it? You know, balancing contribution with salary...Huh? Oh well, let's go on.

Now, let's look at total compensation (It takes more than just salary to satisfy the greed of top management.) According to Rule Two, each level makes double what the next lower level makes. This is a little trickier, but bear with me. Each organizational level gets everything the previous level got, plus something more. It's kind of like a Chinese menu. You know, "With four you get eggroll." Starting with the Supervisor level, let's check it out.

Corporate Lunacy

ACME COMPENSATION STRUCTURE

POSITION	SALARY	OTHER COMP.	TOTAL COMP.
Supervisor	$28,000	($3,000)	$25,000
Manager [a]	$46,000	$4,000	$50,000
Assistant VP [b]	$78,000	$22,000	$100,000
VP [c]	$130,000	$70,000	$200,000
Senior VP [d]	$215,000	$185,000	$400,000
Executive VP [e]	$360,000	$440,000	$800,000
President [f]	$600,000	$1,000,000	$1,600,000
Chairman [g]	$1,000,000	$2,200,000	$3,200,000

a.   Receives previous level benefits, plus retirement savings plan.
b.   Add bonus.
c.   Add stock options.
d.   Add auto, insurance policies and weak long-term plan.
e.   Add enhanced long-term plan and club memberships.
f.   Augment with other good stuff.
g.   Enhance with unspecified benefits and other.

Chapter 4 - Getting Your Share

Now, that's more like it! The Executive VP's total compensation is thirty-two times the Supervisor's, the President thirty-two times the Manager's and the Chairman makes thirty-two times what the Assistant VP makes.

A rather pedestrian compensation scheme has now become a masterpiece! If you think this is fanciful, you might want to pick up the proxy statements of a few corporations. You will see that the rules work for the guys at the top.

Remember Ebeneezer Scrooge? Well, the rapacious old snot was making about $1,000,000 as the boss, while Bob Cratchet was making about $18,000 without benefits (in today's dollars). How the world has changed! Due to its much larger size, the firm now pays Cratchet – the Assistant VP and Controller – a total compensation of $100,000. Scrooge makes a cool $3,200,000.

Bob Cratchet's lot in life improved, but not because Scrooge had a change of heart. Cratchet's better off because the corporation created three compensation levels below him. Scrooge justifies his own compensation package to the shareholders by the fact that there are now four levels between him and Cratchet.

What is the moral of this story? If you want to make more filthy lucre, you really don't have to depend on your own dubious merits. Your avarice can be served by simply arguing that your company needs more compensation levels. This will not only aid you; it will help everyone above you, too, so the suggestion is sure to win immediate approval.

Remember, solidify your position by hiring more people

Corporate Lunacy

and recommending a larger package of perks for your boss. Trickle down works.

EXECUTIVE PERKS AND INCENTIVES – Big "I", Little "u"

"Whenever you accept our views we shall be in full agreement with you."
Moshe Dayan (1915-81)

Perks are important to the mental health of those who have them. How can I feel good, if u and I have the same stuff? How can other people know that MY job is bigger than yours is? Perks, that's how! Perks are more important than money. Unless salaries are prominently published, they don't quite say "mine is bigger" the way a good perk does.

We are talking about a lot more than the key to the executive washroom here. I get to park in the garage, where it's warm in the winter. u must shovel off snow in the employee parking lot. I get a company-paid membership to a country club. u don't get squat. I get a company-paid car, while u don't. My car is always clean, because it is washed for me. Yours is muddy and covered with dings from the "beaters" that parked too close in the crowded employee lot.

The most important perk, however, is the treatment of personal expenses. Axiom: The higher you are in the corporation, the greater the share of your personal expenses that will be paid by the company.

Consider the experience of Freddie Walker, who was promoted to Manager of Forms and Procedures at Blue Sky Industries. Freddie was moved into an office formerly occupied by a Senior Manager. This gave Scott Welper, the Senior Vice-President of Office Protocol, an important job to do – cut Freddie down to size. After all, Freddie, a mere manager, was not entitled to all that senior manager stuff.

Welper replaced the wooden desk used by the office's former occupant with a tasteful, somewhat smaller, brown steel desk. A vinyl-covered steel armchair supplanted the high-backed leather chair. The wood-framed, 24" x 36" genuine imitation of a masterpiece was displaced by a 15" x 20" paint by numbers picture in an aluminum frame.

The couch was removed, and a steel sidechair was put in its place. The real rubber plant, cared for by a plant service, became a fake plastic fern requiring no maintenance. The wooden wastebasket turned into a tin trashcan.

Welper carefully measured the office and determined that it was too big for a manager-level position. So, the carpenters were called in to move the wall back two feet, at a cost of $10,000. The locking door was taken and replaced with a non-locking variety with non-privacy glass. The carpet was removed and replaced with vinyl flooring. The credenza became a steel table.

All the Senior Manager stuff was taken to a warehouse to await the appointment of the next Senior Manager, but there wasn't enough storage space, so it was given away. The cost of

Corporate Lunacy

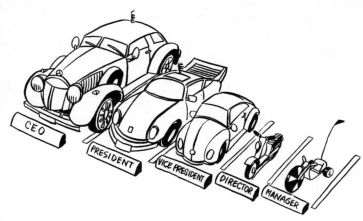

these changes was a mere $39,715.37. But most importantly, Welper's vigilance was instrumental in fending off a potential violation of the hierarchy of perks.

Company cars offer a wonderful opportunity to create distinctions among worthy executives. A Mercedes, BMW, or a Lexus represent appropriate choices for top officials. A Cadillac or a Lincoln is only to be driven by the next most senior executives. A Buick, Mercury or a Chrysler is apropos for vice presidents. A Ford or Chevy work for the next level down, and so on.

If you are issued a Yugo, you should have an idea of where *u* rank. Of course, even a Yugo can be driven proudly past most other employees, because they get nothing, zilch, zippo, *nada*.

The car's accessories are important too. Leather seats have real status. A CD player with the optional home symphony sound package with twelve speakers tells a story. A moon-roof says success like nothing else.

Access to the company limousine absolutely shrieks success. Lester Forsythe (Executive Vice President of Big Chair-Filled Rooms) just loved that uniformed driver running around the car to dutifully open the door.

When Forsythe and his team flew to the big city, he sat in first class by himself while the others sat in the back of the plane. You can rest assured that his colleagues felt proud to be associated with someone of Forsythe's stature.

Access to a company airplane says you've moved up to the top of the status heap. At cocktail parties, when someone is complaining about a long commercial flight delay, think of the jealousy you'll arouse as you smugly say, "That used to upset me, but I only ride the company plane now." You don't have to tell them that the plane available to you is a Piper Cub, and that it takes you about fourteen hours to fly from New York to Chicago. Just drop the name of the pilot and you'll be a big hit.

Note that there is a difference in status between those who can go where the plane is going and those who are able to tell the plane where to go and at what time. If you can use the plane to move some furniture to your Bahamas get-away condo, I would guess that you're basically at the top of the heap.

Dave Lugner (Blue Sky's CEO) made sure that he had a world-class plane to transport him in style. He got the Board to approve a new Grumman V for Blue Sky. The plane cost a mere $35 million and it was well worth it as far as Lugner was concerned. Frankly, it had been embarrassing to fly to the Master's at Augusta in that Citation II.

Corporate Lunacy

All junior executives complain privately about senior executive perks. That's because they feel small and wish they could feel big. However, there's always someone with fewer perks around somewhere. So, even the junior executives can play their own game of big *I* and little *u*.

You probably don't understand any of this if your assigned parking space is more than one-half mile from your office. Those of you who dwell in cubicles may not even know what we're talking about. But, frankly Scarlett…we who have perks don't give a damn!

YOU HAVE A RIVAL – Watching Your Back Isn't Paranoia.

"Even a paranoid can have enemies."
Henry Kissinger (b. 1923)

Chapter 4 - Getting Your Share

And then there was your hated rival, Steve Bowler...arrived at Acme the same week you did...always knew how to dress for any occasion...got his first promotion one month to the day after you got yours. Steve had unnerving cool and always managed to convey the impression that he was class and you were dog meat.

Of course, Steve could also be a little creepy at times. That dawned on you the day you found him crouching in your office with a tape measure. He was simply making sure that his recent promotion had netted him all the square footage he had coming.

At the same time, the guy just oozed charm. In less time than it takes a lawyer to send you a bill, he had wound the boss's gatekeeper around his finger tighter than a wedding band. He even turned the charm on you, when you already knew by intuition, observation and confidential report that he was a son of a...Didn't matter...the third time he asked you out to lunch with that warm, concerned look in his eyes, citing the need to mend fences and build bridges, you finally had to go.

Wow, could he turn it on. After forty minutes he had you convinced that it was only a matter of time before you became CEO...and, in the meantime, would you be his mentor?

He wanted to know how you accomplished the things you did in your department. How did you get such great results? Running the Planning Department must be really hard! Well no, Steve, it's like this...It must have been that second glass of

Corporate Lunacy

wine that made you forget P.T. Barnum's astute observation that there's one born every minute.

A few months and four or five convivial lunches later, Oberstar went into one of his cost cutting spasms. Turning to you and Steve, he requested that each of you eliminate one position from your organization.

Although your Planning Department was already spread thin, you dutifully turned in a suggested reduction. Steve, on the other hand, told Oberstar that his Accounting Department was so tight that it was impossible to cut. However, he did have a creative suggestion that, after a few moments of uncharacteristic virginal reluctance, he finally unveiled for the boss.

He hadn't wanted to mention it because you were such a nice guy, but if Oberstar folded your Planning Department into his Accounting Department, he knew of three positions in your organization that could be cut. And then, of course, they might as well cut you.

As Steve informed the by-this-time fully awake Oberstar, he had extensive experience in planning; and besides, "Planning is mostly numbers anyway." If accepted, Steve's ingenious proposal would eliminate one high-paid position (yours) as well as three low-paid positions.

Steve's plan certainly had merits. Even you could see that. You often wondered why Oberstar didn't go for it. Maybe it was because he had scribbled your name down on the list of half a dozen promising young executives he sent to the Chairman every Christmas. It would have looked a little peculiar firing you four months later. Whatever the reason, Oberstar ultimately told Steve to cut the crap and cut a staff member like he was originally told to do.

Perhaps it was your Frosty-the-Snowman manner that alerted Steve to the fact that you had not been amused by his suggestion. In a rare burst of sensitivity, he stopped issuing luncheon invitations. In a rare burst of self-control, you didn't cram his front teeth back through his glottal cavity.

The cold war continued for about six months. You noticed that when you walked into a room where Steve was talking to other executives, the conversation would often come abruptly to a stop. Was this supposed to make you paranoid? Kind of childish, wasn't it?...Or was it?

Just before Christmas,...it was that really cold December, remember?...you got to work one morning and discovered that Steve had parked in your favorite parking spot. You reclaimed your spot by getting to work earlier the next day. But the following day he was back in your spot again. By golly, this got the testosterone going. He was messing with your stuff. You arrived still earlier the next day and recovered your space. The next morning he was there again. You thought, "Is this guy willing to get up in the middle of the night just to get my spot?" You bet!

Are you willing to take this lying down? Better not. It's 4:15 in the morning. Time to get up and shave and head off to work...

Chapter 4 - Getting Your Share

Welbly would always find time for a little planning

Corporate Lunacy

5 WHY WASTE TIME WORKING

When you could be busy wasting time

If you want to hear the happy sound of committees concocting imaginary universes out of little bits of string, wrapping paper, gumballs and fragments of last year's accounting report, you've come to the right place. Who knows, with enough imagination, you may even get the job of convincing the shareholders that the earth is flat. Somebody's got to do it.

THE MISSION STATEMENT – Fiddling While Rome Burns!

"A man who has peddled twenty-five thousand miles on a stationary bicycle has not circled the globe."
Paul Eldridge

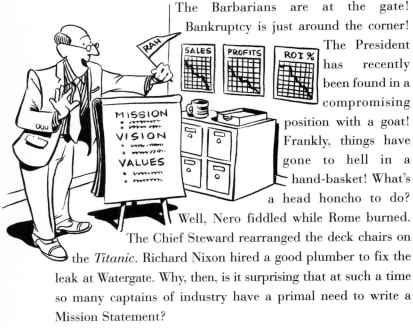

The Barbarians are at the gate! Bankruptcy is just around the corner! The President has recently been found in a compromising position with a goat! Frankly, things have gone to hell in a hand-basket! What's a head honcho to do? Well, Nero fiddled while Rome burned. The Chief Steward rearranged the deck chairs on the *Titanic*. Richard Nixon hired a good plumber to fix the leak at Watergate. Why, then, is it surprising that at such a time so many captains of industry have a primal need to write a Mission Statement?

George Welbly, the ineffectual CEO of Acme Corporation, knew all his peers had a Mission Statement. These statements all seemed so penetrating and philosophical. Welbly wanted to be viewed as a deep thinker by his fellow CEOs. So Welbly, who had run out of ideas for managing his company, decided Acme needed a Statement of Mission. He wanted the best, most profound Mission Statement ever.

Welbly called Les Forsythe, his trusted Executive Vice President in Charge of Big Chair-Filled Rooms, to help him. Forsythe, who thought a mission statement would be a colossal waste of time, naturally expressed to Welbly the intense interest and excitement the prospect of working on this document aroused in him.

Forsythe dutifully gathered as much research on mission statements as he could find. He spent many hours poring through manuals and studying other company's statements. He discovered that all mission statements:

A. Take years to perfect.

B. Go through countless iterations.

C. Divert the attention of the organization from its real business.

D. Have nothing to do with how the organization really functions.

E. Are so general that they could be used by a department store, garage, fast-food restaurant, condom maker, hotel or the US Senate.

He also discovered something even more fascinating. It was as if he had gone to the top of some remote mountain in Tibet and learned an eternal truth from the all-wise guru: "All mission statements use exactly the same 27 words. Only the order of the words is unique."

139

Forsythe took the 27 immutable words and organized them into three columns:

TABLE OF MISSION STATEMENT WORDS

COLUMN A	COLUMN B	COLUMN C
Boldly	Pursue	Mission
Safeguard	Strategic	Vision
Create	Mutual	Values
Achieve	Global	Leadership
Assure	Integrity	Employees
Reward	Responsible	Teamwork
Proactively	Serve	Customers
Imperative	Candid Communications	Shareholders
Provide	Safe and Healthful	Environment

This made it easy for Forsythe to craft a Mission Statement for Welbly. No need to ponder prodigiously. He just used the words, three at a time – one from column A, one from column B, one from column C. Forsythe made sure he used all the words. Then he added a few words to tie it all together. What follows was the final result:

Corporate Lunacy

ACME INDUSTRIES MISSION STATEMENT

We at Acme Industries will boldly pursue our mission.

In doing so, we will safeguard the strategic vision of the corporation. We will create mutual values within the company and achieve global leadership in our businesses. We will assure integrity among our employees and reward them for responsible teamwork.

We intend to always proactively serve our customers.

It is imperative that we maintain candid communications with our shareholders. Finally, we are passionate about the need to provide a safe and healthful environment for the good of mankind.

Chapter 5 - Why Waste Time Working

Voila, Welbly had his Mission Statement! He was so delighted that he instructed each of the company's divisions to create their own Mission Statement. Then all employees were required to construct Personal Mission Statements. Pretty strong medicine for what ailed Acme, don't you think?

Unfortunately, all this frenetic activity caused normal business to almost grind to a halt. Production slowed; product was shipped late; orders were not billed. Salesmen couldn't sell much while they were distracted with writing their statements.

Finally, all the Mission Statements were ceremoniously placed in the new Corporate Policy Manual. Employees dutifully filed the manual away. It was never read, referred to, or considered again. Eventually, people went back to work and Acme survived the experience.

If you must get involved with creating a corporate mission statement, there are a few things to remember:

1. **The whole exercise is futile.** If the boss is looking for a mission and vision, he really needs a clue and a plan.
2. **Be serious.** Do not disparage the effort. The boss thinks it's important. Speak in reverent, positive tones.
3. **Create your own 27-word chart.** Write the words on separate pieces of paper, put them in a jar and shake it up. Draw them one at a time to make your own chart.

Corporate Lunacy

You don't have to use the words in the order presented on Forsythe's list. In fact, that's plagiarizing! Create your own table, but use the same words. Now when CEOs compare Mission Statements, you can play along: "You show me yours, and I'll show you mine."

THE STRATEGIC PLAN – Delusions and Fantasies

"Picture yourself in a boat on a river with tangerine trees and marmalade skies."
John Lennon (1940-80)

Remember how much fun it was to play with your toy Knights of the Roundtable? They always won. They slew the dragon and conquered the evil prince. You built or knocked down castles at will. The bully who kicked sand in your face was vanquished. All of your dreams were realized. Your make-believe world was secure, until your little sister flushed Sir Lancelot down the toilet, or your dog, Sparky, ate Sir Guile.

Most of us are forced to grow up and relinquish playing with action figures eventually. Adults who fantasize are often locked up in asylums, but in the modern corporation these same people become CEOs. Their flights of fancy and exercises in denial are called The Five-Year Plan. Are competitors eating your lunch and kicking sand in your face? Are the workers trying to unionize? Are your shareholders in revolt? No problem! Just like the evil prince, they can be vanquished by the Strategic Plan.

Denial is perfectly acceptable in corporate America as long as it takes the form of a Strategic Plan. Business may just stink, but the plan promises the future will be otherwise. The actual losses of today must give way to high profits tomorrow. After all, a good strategic plan allows the boss to balance the present, which is unacceptable, with a future that is impossible.

Norm Traumer, the CEO of Probe Enterprises, had a problem. Probe's principal business, the production and sale of the Nutpick, was faltering. At one time, Probe had controlled over sixty percent of the Nutpick market. However, under Traumer's leadership, market share had plummeted to less than twenty percent. Worse, the product had become a commodity, pricing had deteriorated, and the Board of Directors was concerned.

Traumer turned to Ted Potsworth, his head wizard, to help him design a Strategic Plan for the Nutpick Division. Traumer knew that Potsworth could make problems disappear in a magical tapestry of big-picture thinking. He could baffle the Board with his bewildering bullshit. He was a master of obfuscation, using multicolored charts, four-quadrant diagrams and share-momentum graphs.

Traumer didn't like the future portrayed by the initial Plan, so Dudley Cox (the senior accountant) just changed the numbers. Massive books filled with future quarterly results expressed to five decimals were assembled. Then Traumer and Potsworth presented their visionary Strategic Plan for the Nutpick Division to the Board.

Corporate Lunacy

The Plan called for aggressively gaining market share, increasing prices and margins, and turning assets faster. (Traumer and Potsworth must have assumed that competitors would either go on vacation or go to sleep). It concluded that an unprecedented level of customer service would restore Probe to a position of market leadership.

Well, it didn't exactly work out that way. Sales remained flat, although Probe began producing any type of Nutpick a customer could conjure up. No order was too small, no request too bizarre. Sterling silver Nutpicks were produced for the high end of the market. One customer wanted ivory Nutpicks, another wanted teakwood from Madagascar. Probe produced plastic Nutpicks in any color the customer wanted. Inventories soared, the number of items stocked rose, and costs escalated. Profits dropped like a stone!

Probe's Quarterly Earnings Report contained the bad news. Actual results were far worse than anticipated. Traumer screamed, "Actual can't be right. The numbers must be wrong. Where is that little weasel accountant, Dudley?"

Unfortunately, the numbers were right. The Nutpick business stunk! The Board heard all the usual excuses for non-attainment – the market had changed, competitors were to blame, the weather had turned bad, etc.

Traumer concluded that a new Strategic Plan with a prediction of an even rosier future was needed. He closed his eyes real tight, turned around three times, clicked his heels and wished real, real hard for things to get better. Then he fired Dudley, the accountant, and Kramer, the Vice President of Nutpick marketing.

He told the board that the Nutpick business had become a commodity and they should approve a new strategic plan for the business. He proposed a write-off of assets, an organizational restructuring, a downsizing and a plan to sell the Nutpick business. The Board awarded Traumer a special bonus for his strategic leadership and aggressive management.

If your boss wants to do some strategic planning, recognize his deep-seated, almost primal, need to do this stuff, then:

1. **Brush up on your buzzwords.** Learn about those bubble-charts, share-momentum graphs, four-quadrant diagrams and core competencies.
2. **Get out your hockey stick.** The Plan is the place for optimism – no room for a nay-sayer here.
3. **Beware of consultants.** They will tell you that your company can be something that it isn't. Were consultants the reason why blue-blood Morgan Guaranty (the most prestigious bank in the world) decided it didn't want to be a bank? It has been adrift now for a decade trying to become an investment bank, something it isn't. And who talked the Internal Revenue Service into trying to become our helpful friend?
4. **If you must construct your own plan...**A hard worker with a mediocre plan will beat a genius who dreams about his exquisite plan every time.

Corporate Lunacy

THE OFFSITE MEETING – What do you mean boondoggle?

"My way of joking is to tell the truth. It's the funniest joke in the world."

George Bernard Shaw (1856-1950)

So you've been invited to an offsite meeting, away from the pressures of the office. Will it be a boondoggle? It won't if you are among the unwashed masses of those who work. However, if you are an executive, you can expect an intensive opportunity to socialize and relax. The higher your level, the less business you will conduct. If you are in senior management, the company will spend more on you than the combined annual salary of all those who report to you.

Consider the Behemoth Company, which has about 20,000 employees. Contrast the differences in the offsite activities available to its various groups of employees.

I. Skills Training for People Who Work.

About 15,000 workers (three-quarters of the employees) belong to this group. The company will spend $10 on each of them for the offsite meeting. The total budget will be $150,000. These low dwellers in the food chain will be treated to Harassment Training run by the Human Resources Department.

For these people, offsite means away from their desks, in a conference room down the hall. The three-hour meeting will

147

include a brown-bag lunch with lemonade or coffee. Each participant will receive a loose-leaf notebook filled with legal jargon outlining the penalties for transgressions. Meeting content will focus on whether summary dismissal, loss of pension, or jail awaits those who do wrong.

II. Indoctrination for Supervisors.

This gathering embodies about 3,000 supervisors. The company will spend $50 on each for a total budget of, again, $150,000. This will be an ISO 9000 Training Session, taught by an outside expert on filling out reports. Those in attendance are expected to take copious notes. The meeting will actually be offsite (at the local YMCA). It will be a one-half day session. Included is a $9.95 buffet lunch (with choice of non-alcoholic beverage) and a round of miniature golf.

III. Seminar for Middle Managers.

This assemblage involves approximately 600 employees. The company will spend $250 per head. Guess what? The total budget is still $150,000. See the pattern? There are one-fifth as many people involved and five times the per-person cost. The purpose is a Strategic Plan Communication Seminar. This meeting will include two nights at a Holiday Inn, no more than 40 miles from headquarters. There will be three starchy meals per day (plus beer). Included is one round of golf on a community course, valued at $20 (not to include a cart). A buffet dinner featuring rubbery chicken, scalloped potatoes and canned string beans at $19.95 per head closes the event.

IV. Team Building for Vice Presidents.

This gathering will embrace about 120 aspirants and cost about $1,250 each. The total budget is $150,000. Location is selected based on weather; Phoenix is nice during the cold winter months. The resort is Camelback or something comparable. Golf will be at a premier course with a cart. The food will be good and include red or white house-wine, your choice. There will be an interesting after-dinner speaker, on a current business topic.

Dress casually for the morning meetings; you will need to move quickly to the golf course. Afternoons will be your own. There will be a welcome buffet dinner and cocktails. The second day will start with a 9:00 A.M. meeting, lasting three hours with two half-hour breaks. Then you'll move on to lunch and recreation. Cocktails will be at seven and dinner at eight. The next day will be more of the same. Leave the following morning unless you want to stay for personal time (the company will pay).

V. Senior Management Strategy Review.

Here we have a stellar collection of 25 worthy souls. The cost is $7,250 per individual (including spouse). The total budget will be, surprise – $150,000! Some might call this a "boondoggle," but it is simply a reward for hard-working executives and a chance for them to do some high-level sucking up. What, you think this is the definition of boondoggle? How silly!

Transportation to and from a world-class resort runs about $1,000. Be sure to pack more clothes for a three-day offsite than you would for ten days in Europe. A room for three days costs $1200. Meals are $700 (including vintage wine selections and cognac). Limo cost is $220 and gifts, $120. That welcome fruit basket is $90. Combined recreation is $600. At this rate it doesn't take long to spend the allotted $7,250 per couple. I'll just take the money, thank you!

If you are lucky enough to be invited to this "meeting," you will play golf on some of the most expensive courses in the nation. Most real people can't afford to play golf at $250 a pop, including greens' fees, caddies, tips, etc. Just don't tell Stan Bobble, the Chairman and CEO, that he can't have a ten-foot gimme putt or shouldn't cheat at croquet.

The speakers will broaden your horizons with a discussion of world affairs rather than talking about business. Wasn't it nice that both George Bush and Mikail Gorbachev could attend? Too bad Maggie Thatcher had a previous engagement.

There will be the mandatory black-tie dinner with the gold service and white-gloved waiters. Although black tie affairs are usually charities looking for big-buck contributions, this time it's the executives who are on the receiving end of charity. Wouldn't you like to take this moment to thank all Behemoth's shareholders? Do you feel a real bond with the management team? I'd rather stay in my room!

Corporate Lunacy

VI. Top Management Customer Trip.

There are five meritorious super incumbents in the inner circle. Their offsite meeting will cost about $36,250 each. In addition, each high roller is encouraged to bring five key contacts. The total budget is five times $150,000.

Oh! Oh! We broke the pattern, but what the hell... the purpose is to solidify key strategic relationships. How about a safari in Africa, followed by a 14-day cruise to the Orient? Jetting home on the Concorde might add a special touch. Alternatively, why not play all the famous Scottish golf courses, coupled with a stay at each important Scottish castle. Trout fishing in Greenland might also be swell.

VII. The Chairman Speaks with God.

This rendezvous includes one key individual, Stan Bobble, @ $150,000. Total budget is $150,000 (plus whatever else Stan wants). The purpose is Intense Ego-Building Activities. This meeting will be held whenever and wherever Stan desires. It will consist of whatever he wants. Do you have a problem with that?

If you are even slightly perceptive, it's easy to tell if you rate in a corporation based on the meeting you attend. Are you getting the bag lunch or the gold-service gourmet feast? Does the topic have to do with business? How high is the work/play ratio? Is the location a conference room or a posh resort? If you look around and all the other attendees are from the mailroom, you know where you stand.

THE ANNUAL REPORT – Obfuscation and Evasiveness.

"The crime is not that Nero played while Rome burned, but that he played badly."
Ned Rorem (1923-)

The Annual Report is supposed to be a company's report card. Ideally, its centerpiece, The Chairman's Letter to Shareholders, will describe what has happened over the year, what dividend was paid to shareholders and what prospects the future holds. In reality, however, it's a truly monumental slog through a mountain of palaver that will give you only a bare inkling of what's going on.

The glossy Annual Report of Blue Sky Industries was one of the trendiest reports published. It was filled with multi-colored charts and graphs and had the theme "People are our most important resource." Dave Lugner, Blue Sky's Chairman, wrote a scintillating letter that focused on Blue Sky's great strategic progress. Unfortunately, the report was misleading at best. Blue Sky was sinking and its earnings were pitiful.

Let's look at Lugner's letter, which we have abbreviated in the interest of keeping you, the reader, awake. Can you figure out what's really happening at Blue Sky?

Chapter 5 - Why Waste Time Working

To our Shareholders:

Although we reported a net loss in 1998, the numbers mask the continued progress we made in implementing our long-term strategic plan. It was a challenging year in many respects, but we had many solid achievements. Importantly, we have maintained our leadership position in key markets. Sales, while a little slow relative to last year, were far higher than they were a decade ago. Foreign subsidiary sales made a special contribution, increasing nearly 50 percent. Our international strategy of expanding small but high-potential businesses is clearly paying dividends.

We advanced a number of important pricing initiatives and have considerable optimism that we will be able to bring a new sense of pricing discipline to the marketplace. We have been aggressively attacking costs, with a well thought-out program oriented around an indepth value creation analysis. Plan shortfalls in some areas have been offset by an assertive program related to overhead costs and inventory. Our strong customer base has allowed us to attain a low level of bad debt.

This New Year brings new opportunity for fresh starts and goal setting. Where are we going? Where have we been? What have we accomplished? Forget all that! We'll do better next year! Success will require hard work, imagination, confidence and going the extra mile. Specifically, we must anticipate trends, identify opportunities, and position ourselves for success. We are "restructuring" our organization and our production configuration to align ourselves with the realities of the marketplace. We are nurturing an entrepreneurial spirit and a greater degree of management focus. We are committed to a standard of excellence regarding health, safety and the environment.

Finally, I wish to thank all our employees who worked long and hard. Truly, these people are the company's most precious asset. Also, I want to thank all our shareholders. It is a privilege to do this work we have been entrusted as your loyal servants.

Dave Lugner
Chairman and CEO
March 1, 1999

OK, so much for the BS and the flowery words. If this guy really wanted to come clean, he might have described Blue Sky's condition as follows:

Corporate Lunacy

To The People Who Are Dumb Enough to Own Our Stock (You must have the collective IQ of printing ink)

Boy, did we ever lose a bunch of money in 1998. We would like to think that it was a year of great strategic progress. However, there is no evidence to support that view. The year stunk, and the only thing solid we achieved was blockhead status. We continue to be the only company interested in producing the tired products we try to sell. Sales fell far short of budget because we were all golfing rather than selling. Who believes in budgets anyway? Sales benefited from pre-delivery recognition, special promotions and gifts recorded as sales. Foreign subsidiary sales (even though they didn't amount to much) were up 50 percent, excluding figures we didn't like. Expanding these "piss-ant" businesses may pay us dividends, but they won't pay you. We have stopped paying shareholders a cash dividend.

Pricing has remained flat since antediluvian times. Our last price increase announcement was greeted by laughter. Our costs are out of control, particularly for executive expenses. The strong cost control measures we discuss may finally offset weak pricing...in about the fourth quarter of 2012. Shortfalls from our plans were largely offset by accounting changes. We understated cost of goods sold with respect to the amount of overhead costs held in inventory. Bad debt reserves were reduced from $5 million to a negative $4 million. I don't know what a negative bad debt implies, but it added $9 million to income.

The action plans for improving our performance consist of: 1. Strong prayer, 2. Marginal analysis to determine the trade off between hope and despair, and 3. Self-abnegation, whatever that is. Our "restructuring" will consist of firing one low-paid secretary and writing off some old inventory. We use buzzwords like managerial focus and entrepreneurial spirit and talk about excellence regarding health, safety and the environment to lay smoke over our lack of activity.

As I mentioned earlier, our employees (laughingly called our most precious asset) spent most of their time on the golf course, spending your money. If any of you shareholders figure out how this company is really doing...keep it to yourself. I need the job!

Dave Lugner
Chairman and CEO
March 1, 1999

Chapter 5 - Why Waste Time Working

Well, you say, "Maybe Lugner's letter is misleading, but at least the independent auditors will tell us what is really going on." Are you kidding? The boilerplate Report of the Independent Auditors is sterile and vapid. It is as exhilarating as a ballet recital and tells nothing about the condition of Blue Sky. In fact, this year's Report is an exact replica of last year's, but it still took the not-so-independent auditors three months, and several hundred thousand dollars, to produce.

Maybe it's too much to ask the auditors to expose Lugner for the fraud he is. They would be fired and lose their fat fees. But couldn't they at least give a creative and original report? How about producing a kinder and gentler audit letter? A letter that would meet the highest standards of irrelevance but still be fun:

Corporate Lunacy

Report of Not-So-Independent Auditors

To the Shareholders, Board of Directors and Friends of the Blue Sky Company:

We have browsed through the fine balance sheet of the Blue Sky Company as of December 31,1998 and 1997. Looks good to us! Related stuff such as income, shareholders' equity and cash flow have been judged for originality, neatness and clarity. We take no responsibility for the statements or for their accuracy. Our responsibility is to express a boilerplate bunch of words which can be used in the annual report. While this is called an "opinion," we will quickly cover our tracks if the company gets in trouble or is faced with any legal action.

We conducted our audit in accordance with the way most auditors do this stuff. We tried to find any small misstatements that would not jeopardize our fee. Our examinations involved countless hours of work and substantial expense. We would like to thank all those who toiled so long and hard to produce this outstanding result. Although we know nothing about the business, we went through all the tests of accounting records we could think of. We computed innumerable ratios that, while fascinating, were not illuminating.

In our opinion, the financial statements and other stuff referred to above present quite a picture of the financial position of the Company. They do this in the finest obfuscating language. At December 31, 1998, the company appears well balanced. They have explained all the changes in their financial condition that we could comprehend. We have a strong suspicion that they conform to generally accepted accounting principles and have shown great originality and initiative.

PEEK, MARVEL and MISSIVE

New York, NY
February 20, 1999

So, what the heck should you do with those boring annual reports? You know now that they are basically bullshit. However, if you insist on trying to learn something from these tedious tomes, remember the following:

1. If the report is geared to a rosy future, it means the present is just awful.
2. The longer the report, the less its substance.
3. Compare what you know happened in the company to the words in the report.
4. Have fun. The annual report will probably be the funniest stuff you've ever read.

THE ANNUAL MEETING – A Cure for Insomnia!

"Meetings are indispensable when you don't want to do anything."
John Kenneth Galbraith (1908-)

The SEC requires public corporations to hold annual meetings of their shareholders. However, they can't direct companies to make them interesting or convenient.

Shareholders ask embarrassing questions about management compensation, strategy and spending. They want to know about earnings, dividends and the stock price. They are, quite frankly, pests! They want management to be accountable for its actions. Therefore, there are only about nine public companies that really want shareholders to attend their meetings.

Corporate Lunacy

George Welbly of the Acme Corporation wasn't a misanthrope, he just suffered from Shareholder Avoidance Syndrome (SAS). This affliction caused him to select remote sites for his annual meetings. Bismarck, North Dakota, in the winter and Bartlesville, Oklahoma, in the summer were good choices. Like many reclusive captains of industry, he thought Canal Fulton, Ohio, was really swell.

Shouldn't a CEO suffering from SAS be given the sympathy accorded to others who suffer from a syndrome? Your sister's kid can't be called a pain-in-the-butt...he has Attention Deficit Disorder (ADD). And your lazy brother-in-law...Chronic Fatigue Syndrome (CFS).

New York City would seem to be a surprising choice for Behemoth's annual meeting. However, Stan Bobble chose a hotel that was fifteen blocks from the nearest subway stop. It was large and had only one working elevator. Its meeting room was fourteen stories up, and the sign for it was hidden behind a tree in the lobby. New York hotel personnel could always be counted on to be surly and uncommunicative, but just to be sure, he would hold his meeting just before or just after a holiday.

At the Behemoth Annual Meeting there were eighty-six attendees: twelve company directors, twenty-five company officers, six company auditors, ten bankers, eight investment bankers, five proxy solicitors, six company secretaries, five security guards, two annual meeting gadflies, three shareholders and a partridge in a pear tree. There were also four unemployed, retired or otherwise unoccupied people.

Chapter 5 - Why Waste Time Working

The inspectors of election read their report – scintillating stuff! The Corporate Secretary droned on about votes for, against, abstentions, percentages, etc. There was a proposal to approve a richer stock plan for management. There were motions and seconds and more motions, all made by company officers. Bobble made a boring speech rivaling one of Castro's eight-hour marathon talks.

Finally, the time came for questions from the floor. One old lady stood and complained about the quality of the donuts (her husband had his plastic-lined pockets full). One retiree stood and complained that current management was ruining the company. Then the corporate gadfly prattled on for forty-five minutes. He didn't care about answers, he just wanted to hear himself talk.

Those distinguished looking board members were sitting on the platform with Bobble for one reason – MONEY! They made $50,000 a year plus $2,000 for each meeting that they attended. Their travel was paid, their insurance provided, and they received retirement pensions, stock plans, etc. Their primary job was to listen to boring presentations and speak only in a supportive way. They didn't need the wisdom of Solomon, just the patience of Job! They sat for hours listening to boring presentations, to boring presentations, to boring...HELLO, did I wake you?

Bobble's board was careful to show "diversity" by having a token woman and a minority member. I'm afraid that their definition of diverse was not very diversified.

Corporate Lunacy

The Behemoth meeting was incredibly expensive. Company personnel and board members were flown in on a fleet of executive and company airplanes. And they didn't stay at the Holiday Inn, Airport. Try the Pierre. They all arrived four days early and stayed two extra days. They took in three plays, the symphony and a Knick's game. Of course the company paid – silly! Dinner at Burger King? NOT! Would you believe a banquet for twenty at the Four Seasons?

So, you think you really want to go to an Annual Meeting? If you are an insomniac, I highly recommend it. If you are there for any other reason – get a life!

Ralph figured a nap was probably out of the question.

Corporate Lunacy

6 THINGS AND STUFF

I know you're wondering if this is where I talk about all the stuff I couldn't shoehorn into any of the other sections. Of course it is.

THE NEW OFFICE BUILDING

"Vanity dies hard; in some obstinate cases it outlives the man."
Robert Louis Stevenson (1850-94)

Stan Bobble, the Chairman and CEO of the Behemoth Corporation, was worried that no one would remember him. "Wouldn't it be tragic if people don't recall my name, let alone my face? A simple oil portrait in the boardroom won't do. Who would see it, except the board members? Besides, most of the time the boardroom is dark. That new Mission Statement is pretty dynamic, but the company needs something that shouts Bobble...something original, enlightened and solid." Then, inspiration struck the Chairman like a left hook! "We need to erect a new office building!"

So, Bobble presented his idea for a new headquarters to the Board of Directors. "The Behemoth Company deserves a home that makes an important statement. A great company like ours should have a headquarters that is consistent with its reputation. Under my leadership, Behemoth has become a treasured name in the hearts of our customers. The cost of this powerful statement should be only about $50 million."

The Board just nodded agreement. Stotz and Evans went back to sleep; Browning asked when lunch would be served; and Arnold asked if he could be paid in cash rather than by check. "Then it's settled; we are building our bridge to the 21st century. Meeting adjourned."

Corporate Lunacy

Planning the building gave Bobble something to do when he wasn't in Washington or out on the golf course. Besides, the board had a distraction from sales and earnings, which were going down the drain.

Bobble selected you, his VP of Manipulation and Rearrangement, to spearhead the project. You had an opportunity to suck up to good old Stan. You also had a chance to be a spear-catcher rather than spear-header. Were you going to be the one to tell him that this prospective erection was foolish and unnecessary? I don't think so!

Site Selection.

First, a site for the new building had to be found. Although you did exhaustive research to find a site, you would have little to do with the final selection. Bobble would do that. Generally, a new headquarters will be close to the boss's home. However, Stan's marriage was rocky. A long commute was called for.

Bobble was insistent that a qualified commercial broker be involved in the location search. It just happened that Bobble knew an excellent broker – Sally, his girlfriend. Are you surprised that the long commute puts the new headquarters close to her apartment?

Selecting an architect.

Selecting an architect was the next decision. As the project head, you reviewed the recommendations of those who were knowledgeable. You diligently studied the past and current projects of various architects. You assessed their creativity, weighed by time and cost. You determined the adequacy of their staff to support engineering and design.

Finally, you presented your report. Bobble wanted someone of real stature. Too bad I.M. Pei was busy. Oh, by the way, Sally happened to know a terrific architect – her brother Bob. Are you paying attention? OK, maybe you were a wimp, but you recommended the guy and you're still employed.

The design phase.

Architects care only about aesthetics. Bob didn't care if anything worked. He didn't care if the offices were a hundred and ten degrees in the summer and twenty-six degrees in the winter. Bob's vision was to see forever through glass. Offices may be triangular, halls may go nowhere, and doors may not open, but the style is in. Price was no object to Bob. The final cost of all Bob's projects was always at least fifty percent more than his first estimates.

Bobble's office would be the centerpiece of the building. The floor plan accentuated his importance by putting almost everyone else in cubicles rather than offices. The result was a statement making, 250 x 200 ft. chairman's office (complete with conference room, anteroom, private dining room and private bathroom). Of course, this "statement" added another floor to the building.

Then the costs really began to escalate. The architect said, "If you want insulated glass, we must add $565,000." And,

"Oh, you mean you don't want the bathroom on the roof?" – $85,000. "You want commercial grade toilets?" – $234,000.

"Air conditioning that doesn't make you jump when it starts." – $750,000. "Oh, we thought you wanted 200,000 sq. ft. of total space. You mean you wanted 200,000 sq. ft. of office space? Our design includes 100,000 sq. ft. of atriums, halls, stairs, etc., and allows 100,000 sq. ft. for offices. We'll have to increase the total building to 300,000 sq. ft." – That's another $10,000,000. They downsized the offices of middle managers to help offset these costs.

Hiring a decorator.

Next, you hired a decorator (a flamboyant architect with a lisp). Bruce didn't give a damn about cost or function. "Do you want to look like you have no class?" Decorating would cost at least fifty percent more than the original estimate.

Bruce claimed that the antique furniture, authentic Persian rugs and inlaid mahogany paneling were necessities. Because Impressionists make a good impression, he insisted on a number of original masterpieces: Renoir, Monet, Manet and a particularly stunning Degas. These features added $10 million to the project cost, and Bruce convinced Bobble that he really needed them.

Bobble asked cost-conscious you to find a way to pay for them. Finally, it was agreed that these costs could be partly offset by reducing employee cubicle sizes to 6' x 6', from the 12' x 12' originally planned. "Will that cause any morale problem?"

asked Bobble. You bravely said, "I think the employees won't mind, and they will feel real pride when they can look at those authentic masterpieces on visitor's day." Further savings came from using furniture for the cubicles that was freed up by the most recent AT&T downsizing.

Site preparation and construction.

The site excavators destroyed every piece of vegetation and knocked down every tree, even though you hired an armed guard to protect the landscape. This gave the landscapers an opportunity to replace everything but the dirt (after an environmental study). The dirt they covered with mulch. You didn't remind Bobble that the original attraction of the site was that it was wooded. The construction people, who drove pickups with Astroturf in the back, didn't get along with either the architects or the designers.

Staff infighting.

The new building brought out the worst in the Corporate VPs. They jockeyed for prime office space at each other's expense. Most had no problem gouging each other for a few extra square feet.

Why was your rival, Steve Bowler, measuring your office again? Why did he present a plan to move your group to the basement in order to accommodate his people? Why did you as project manager relocate Steve's office next to the men's restroom? That's the breaks, Steve.

Corporate Lunacy

Ringing up the final costs.

The Board approved the modest $50 million cost estimated for the project without an objection. Bobble didn't want to tell them that the final cost was more than fifty percent higher – over $75 million. Instead he told his board that this great institutional erection was on time and under budget.

He focused on the final cost of the building only, compared with the estimate for the total project. Site preparation became environmental testing. The cafeteria, an employee benefit. The architect's crazy ideas became research and development. Contracts with the builders were charged to legal expense. Bobble's office furnishings – goodwill.

All the new artwork – that's a corporate contribution! The parking lot was obviously not part of the building. Moving expense was part of the transportation budget. When all was said and done, the Stan Bobble Building was on time and under budget! (If you believe that, I've got some wooded property in the rain forest that's right for you.)

Some self-righteous moralizing.

Why do most of these projects happen shortly before the company goes belly-up? Because the boss has his eye on the wrong ball, that's why! He says, "What the heck, the company ought to be able to afford a few million bucks, and if the shareholders don't like it, they can stuff it." Bad attitude.

THE CAFETERIA – and the Executive Dining Room

"Let them eat cake!"
Marie Antoinette (1755-93)

You are what you eat! That's why top executives dine differently
than the rest of us. They dine in different places and they eat
different stuff. If Charles Dickens were alive today, his Tale of
Two Cities could have been a novel about the chasm between
the Executive Dining Room and the Employee Cafeteria.

The executives at Widget Industries, Inc. couldn't understand
why the employees were always grumbling about the food. So
what if the Tuna Noodle Surprise was cold. Executives had bigger

problems to worry about! Their truffles weren't fresh, and the Chardonnay was two degrees too warm. Dessert was a disaster! The *Gran Marnier Soufflè* fell, and the presentation of the rest of the food was not up to standard.

Why don't we take a closer look at the contrast between the Executive Dining Room and the Employees' Cafeteria at Widget Industries? There is a huge difference in the cost of an individual meal between the two places. However, the total cost of the Executive Dining Room seems small to Widget management. After all, only twenty-five executives eat in Widget's dining room, while two thousand employees eat in the cafeteria.

WIDGET INDUSTRIES DINING FACILITIES

ITEM	EXECUTIVE DINING ROOM	EMPLOYEE CAFETERIA
Room size	Intimate	Immense
Furnishings	Inlaid Teak	Steel and Formica
Flowers	Orchids	Plastic Roses
Glassware	Waterford Crystal	Paper Cups
Napkins	Belgian Linen	Scotties
Dishes	Lennox	Aluminum Serving Trays
Service	Waiters in Tuxedos	Army Style Chow Line
Food	French Cuisine	Ladles of Stuff
Beverage	Fine Wine	Watery Kool-Aid

Chapter 6 - Things and Stuff

Widget's Executive Dining Room comfortably seats a total of fifty worthy souls in five small, private rooms. The mood of the day is enhanced by the sonorous tones of a Mozart piano concerto wafting pleasingly over the delightful tables, charmingly decorated with fresh orchids. The attentive waiter eagerly anticipates your every want with graceful white-gloved service. Quiet refinement and an air of sophisticated elegance characterize Widget's resplendent dining room. The dining experience is unhurried but attentive. A perfectly styled presentation enhances today's culinary masterpiece. There is a wonderful marriage of the olfactory and visual senses creating that fulfilling enchantment that can only come from exquisite attention to detail.

Now, let's check out Widget's Employee Cafeteria. It's about the size of Yankee Stadium. You can't hear yourself think because of the din of the workers shouting to be heard over the clatter of the mess-hall trays. Elbow your way into the chow line, where you get a scoop of this stuff or a ladle of that stuff. Let your food get cold while you wait for the guy at the cash register to ring you up. Then belly up to a table to eat your slop. Notice that the plastic flowers have three years' dust and grime on them.

Let's look at the menu in Widget's Dining Room: For an appetizer we have our choice of a remarkable *Cervelle De Canut*, the stunning *Tourte Aux Herbes*, or perhaps your palate would be pleased by the striking *Limousine D'Ecrevisses*. For a main course can we show you the highly rated *Thon A La Languedociene*, the sensational *Coq Au Vin*, or perhaps you would like to experience Chef Hubert's favorite, *Cotes De Veau*?

Of course, your plate will be garnished with those perfect accompaniments that are planned to make your dining experience both satisfying and gratifying. For a special treat, you might enjoy the wonderful stuffed zucchini flowers.

Consider a dessert from a titillating selection of delightfully rich *Creme Carmel*, the renowned *Tarte Aux Fraises*, or the sinfully abundant *Meringues A La Chantilly*. Rest assured that the wines have been chosen personally and lovingly from the executive wine cellar by the sommelier. There is a splendid *Bordeaux*, a remarkable yet perky *Chardonnay*, a heady and lusciously viscous and earthy *Cabernet* and the richly intense *Mersault* with subtle hints of tobacco, currants, lemons, herbaceous cuttings and burnt cork. They will perfectly complement and gladden your dining selections and enhance the subtle, yet remarkable, flavors of your gourmet experience.

Hasn't Widget made this culinary adventure a refreshing respite from your hectic morning of important decisions?

Meanwhile, back at the Widget Cafeteria... The Neanderthal ladling out stuff in the chow line is wearing the same kind of latex gloves your doctor wears when he's hell bent on examining your prostate. The soup is overcooked paste, and the chili has a brown crust on it. You can choose Vegetarian Stuffed Bell Pepper, Salmon Patties topped with a white gooey gravy with peas, The Mystery Meat Stew, or (my favorite) the

Tuna Noodle Surprise (Friday's Tuna Noodle Surprise is warmed over excess *Thon A La Languedocienne* from Monday's offering in the Executive Dining Room). At the salad bar, they weigh your plate and charge you by the ounce.

Your lunch can be washed down with either watered-down *Kool-Aid*, or something that resembles iced tea. Top it off with a large helping of lime fluff for dessert. They haven't discovered seasonings in the cafeteria, so you'd better like your food "bland as grandma's rest home." One tip! If you have to choose between beef stew and the stuff that makes its own gravy in the bowl, I recommend the latter.

There you have it. Widget Industries, Inc. believes that executives think executive thoughts because they eat executive food. The rest of you think pedestrian, plodding thoughts because you eat that bland crap in the Employee Cafeteria. You are what you eat!

STRESS AND TECHNOLOGY – Never a Moment's Peace

"We live in an age when unnecessary things are our only necessities."
Oscar Wilde (1854-1900)

People are working fewer hours, according to the U.S. Department of Labor. The average workweek was thirty-nine and a half hours in 1997 versus 42.8 hours in 1948. Some statisticians would note that the average has crept up since the low of thirty-eight hours in 1982. But forget that, okay! This is my story and I'll choose the statistics I want.

Obsessive-compulsive managers who never seem to leave the job affect the trend. You know them. They're the ones whose ringing pagers interrupt your romantic dinner at that little French bistro. They're the ones who disrupt your vacation reverie around the pool at Hilton Head with their loud cell phone conversations. They're the same ones who tie up the pay phone at the airport, e-mailing stuff to their office. Maybe it's not just they. Are you one of them?

These hyper-achieving workers spend between sixty to eighty hours per week at work. They arrive at their office at 7:00A.M. and leave at 7:00P.M. during the week, then put in a leisurely six hours on Saturday...and that's just the time they are physically in the office. They take work home at night and on the weekend. They exercise at the gym with a cell phone at their ear.

They vacation with their laptop. They go to the opera with their pager on their belt. No wonder they only have 1.2 kids per family. They don't have any energy left for sex. American business is losing its competitive edge because it's being run by a bunch of workaholic zombies.

Modern technology has made it possible to never be away from your work. Some people can't go to the john without cackling into the cell phone while they lubricate the plumbing. Downsizing has only exacerbated the trend. These folks are single-handedly trying to do the work of all the people they've canned.

Talk about stress. This kind of lifestyle causes high blood pressure, high cholesterol, hormonal disturbances, poor eating habits, crankiness, weight gain,...heart attack. The higher such people get on the management totem pole, the higher their risk. Premature male menopause and testosterone decline among executives is common. Of course, it's also possible that the primary problem is wearing shorts that are too tight.

STRESS INDUCING TECHNOLOGIES:

E-mail was invented by the devil. Have you ever gone on vacation and found sixty-seven e-mail messages waiting when you returned? They are all marked "highest priority." Then there is the reply loop. You can take the original message, attach your reply and e-mail it back. You get a short reply attached to your reply. You send a reply attached to the reply. Then there is a reply to the reply to the reply...to the reply. HELLO! Can you remember who initiated the whole thing? Of course you can. Back on about page six is the original message.

Voice mail can be infuriating. Don't you just love getting to the office in the morning and hearing all those voice mail messages? Don't those long monologues from the babbling types just frost your cookies? They can't organize their thoughts so they just prattle on, ten minutes or more. If you were actually speaking with them, you could give them a verbal slap in the chops and say, "Get to the point." However, with voice mail, you have to listen to the whole thing in the vain hope that they will eventually say something worthwhile.

Cell phones are insidious. Don't try to hide. They will find you. You could be standing in the middle of a stream fishing for trout and your cell phone will ring. Not only does it scare the fish, it ruins your digestion.

I was recently relaxing on the beach in St. Thomas when some type-A executive talking loudly on his cell phone interrupted my dreams. He was carrying on about some business deal. When he left to go back to his villa, I thought, "Great...some peace and quiet." But he was soon back. He was still on the phone, but he had added a camcorder to his arsenal. Can you believe it? While he was doing a business deal he was also filming how much fun he was having. My sons and I placed our bets on the time of his forthcoming heart attack. But maybe, he couldn't fit the "big one" into his schedule.

Pagers mean you're never out of touch. They are worse than cell phones. They are a call telling you to make a call. ET phone home! Why not just answer your cell phone and skip the extra step? Pagers always go off at exactly the wrong time, like while you are lining up an important putt. They beep at the theater and go off at dinner. Have you ever been in church when one of those things went off in the middle of a prayer? God calling?

Air phones have changed the friendly skies into the chatty skies. One of the few good things about air travel used to be that you could get a little time when "they" couldn't find you. Of course, you had to listen to the flight attendant say for the umpteenth time, "If the mask drops down, fit it around…, etc." Or you had a captain who droned on with a travel guide to the air, pointing out every landmark. You couldn't keep that passenger next to you from giving you his medical history or avoid the screeching kid in the seat in front of you. Okay, I admit that airplanes were always awful. But at least you had some time away from the office. Not any longer! Thanks to air phones, they can find you!

Faxes. It doesn't seem to matter where you are, you can get and receive faxes. You can no longer say, "I'll get to it when I get back to the office." You've got the material, so the boss expects an immediate reply. Every hotel can receive a fax. No more waiting a week or more for the mail. And the new plain paper faxes are easy to read. No more pretending that you can't decipher that rolled up mess of special fax paper.

Laptop Computers. Now you can take your work with you everywhere. You also have a chance to do everything twice when the battery on your laptop fades before you can save your work. What about when the airplane lurches and you slop your wine all over your keyboard? Pssst, fzzzzz and zap…the resulting electrical short scrubs your hard drive. Bad

Corporate Lunacy

phone connections always confound your attempts to send or receive e-mail.

Laptop e-mail. As long as you have a laptop computer, you can send e-mail from any hotel room. You used to be able to think about things before you had to reply. It could be days between correspondence. Now we are talking real time.

Word processing. Remember when you used to be able to take a little rest while you were waiting for a draft of a document to be retyped? Cut and paste and whiteout made making changes difficult. Now, word processing just alters the file on your floppy disk. Damn, those changes come back quickly.

The ease of making changes has caused documents to get longer and more complex. Lawyers, in particular, abuse this. Contracts written for one purpose are easily amended to cover another situation. Attorneys never take anything out; they just add more clauses.

We've seen how technology has increased the amount of stress connected with already high-stress jobs. And stress can kill you – or at least screw up your digestive system. Do you want to avoid doctors, hospitals, rehabilitation? If so, you need to make some changes in your life.

1. **Just say no.** Refuse to use all the technological gadgets. Why not just "forget" your pager occasionally? Oops! I guess you just mistakenly erased that voice mail message.

2. **Claim battery failure.** This allows you to say, "Oh, my cell phone battery went dead so I couldn't receive your call." Or how about, "My computer battery malfunctioned and I just couldn't find a replacement at that scuba diving resort in Belize."

3. **Be a bumbler.** Try destroying the boss's floppy disks a few times. Executives aren't supposed to know much about computers anyway. You can bet that he'll stop trusting you with his files.

4. **Hire an answering service.** At least then they can answer the pager and you won't have to be interrupted at the symphony.

5. **Take your Prozac and your Valium.** Pretty hard to be stressed out when you're drifting on a cloud. Huh? Did I wake you? My, what a nice smile you have.

Corporate Lunacy

MIDDLE MANAGEMENT – Welcome to Purgatory

"He's a real Nowhere Man, sitting in his Nowhere Land, Making all his nowhere plans for nobody. Doesn't have a point of view, knows not where he's going to, Isn't he a bit like you and me?"
John Lennon (1940-80)

Remember when you finally got that promotion you were wanting so much? They made you the Manager of Forms and Procedures – long on title, short on tenure. You became part of middle management. The problem is that middle management is the purgatory of corporate America – admired by no one, despised by all. You used to be able to hide in the obscurity of the masses, but now they can find you.

Once you made middle management, you had to work more hours. Even though they gave you a small raise, on an hourly basis you were making less money because now you had to work fifty to sixty hours per week.

You had all kinds of responsibilities but no authority. If things went wrong, D. A. Mann (your boss) had someone to blame – and, if a sacrifice was necessary, to fire. You were there to do the unpleasant tasks he would rather not do himself. And whenever he compared his perks to yours, it was "I feel superior" time for old D. A.

You lost all the friends you had among your coworkers because you were no longer one of the gang. They began to view you with suspicion. Those who now reported to you actually

Chapter 6 - Things and Stuff

thought you were management.

They despised you because you seemed to have power; they detested you because they thought you were an obstruction to work; and they considered you degenerate because you had a few lousy perks. In short, you had become a worthless slug and perhaps a traitor as well.

Talk about a great way to get a complex! You were stuck in the wasteland. Upper management wouldn't talk to you, but they expected you not to fraternize with the troops. You were like a guy with an MBA from Parma University; you were the appendix of the corporation (no useful function). You were dead center in the food chain, prey for all the big animals. You had too many anxieties to sleep at night. Didn't you just want to run off to some Caribbean island?

Actually you had a lot of company, although maybe you didn't realize it at the time. About fifteen percent of workers are middle managers, and the majority of them are dissatisfied. In fact, everyone below the level of executive management, but above those who work, is middle management. None of these people has power, in spite of all the empowerment nonsense popular today. There is upper-middle management, middle-middle management and lower-middle management. Even executives like Mann thought of themselves as middle management.

In the army, a Second Lieutenant is middle management. He gets about $25 per month more in salary but has to buy his own uniforms (which cost an extra $50 per month). He also must pay for the slop in the mess hall that he used to get for

Corporate Lunacy

free. Worst, he is the guy who gets to lead any frontal assault on enemy lines. This natural downsizing activity occurs whenever the army wants to restructure.

A SHORT HISTORY OF MIDDLE MANAGEMENT

In the beginning, there was a boss with a few workers. He made a bunch of money and wanted to play golf. He hired the first middle manager to watch the workers every afternoon. But soon this manager also wanted to play golf. So more middle managers were hired, and so on.

As work became more complex, specialization created a new group of middle managers. They exist because no one knows what they do. This allows outside specialists, called consultants, to pretend they know what the inside specialists are doing. They then re-engineer the corporation, outsourcing the inside specialists.

THE MIDDLE MANAGEMENT HALL OF FAME

Elmer Fetchit-   invented cold-call-marketing, causing everyone to reject him.

Fred Funk-   founded the first organ bank for appendix donors.

Billy Martin-   was downsized seven times by the same company (the Yankees).

Dennis Rodman-   began dress-down day (cross-dressing, tattoos and multi-colored hair).

Jeffrey Dahmer-   his boss said, "We need more arms and legs to complete this project."

George Custer-   thought he should get closer to the "Indians" in the organization.

Nathan Hale-   who said, "I regret that I only can be downsized once."

Dick Morris -   who said, "I'd rather suck toes than do what the boss wants."

Corporate Lunacy

So, there you were, stuck in middle management, and it did nothing but give you hives. You were an object of ridicule, a scapegoat, cannon-fodder and flotsam. You worked ever harder hoping to finally get that promotion that would elevate you beyond middle management. However, you finally realized that unless you became one of the handful of people who actually ran the place, you would always be middle management. "What should I do," you ask?

1. **Blend into the scenery**. It would be best if you could disguise yourself as a potted palm tree. Remember to duck when the shrapnel starts flying.

2. **Find that unusual (and fictitious) mentor** who will actually take the heat himself.

3. **Appear indispensable** by making your job incomprehensible.

SEX IN THE WORK PLACE

"Sex is one of the nine reasons for reincarnation. The others are unimportant."
Henry Miller (1891-1980)

"Sex, sex, sex, it's all about sex," said James Carville. Well, the White House isn't the only place where sex is a problem. Look at what's happening around you in the corporate work place. Are you disgusted by the degenerate, depraved, wicked, immoral and salacious behavior of some of your coworkers? Are you offended by those cars rocking in the parking lot at noon or by the boffing in the copier room after hours? What about the groping under stairwells or in the utility closet and the fondling behind closed office doors?

Corporate Lunacy

Are you most upset by the simple fact that you aren't getting any? Perhaps, you want a piece of the action, just like you want your fair share of the money and the perks? If you are having sex, wouldn't it be even better if you had a partner to share it with?

Corporate job titles tell the all-consuming nature of sex in the work place. What do you think that Mary, the Director of Community Affairs, really does? Would she be sympathetic if you requested a community affair?

Do you think that John, the Director of Investor Relations, just talks to all those Wall Street security analysts? Or does he take his job more seriously and engage in serious relations? No wonder the stock price is up – all those satisfied investors.

Check out June, the Manager of Governmental Affairs. If those governmental affairs are good enough for Clinton, I guess they're good enough for her. Or Denise, the Vice President of Public Relations – did they add that "l" to public by mistake? When Laurie told you she was Manager of Position Evaluation, did you ask her which one is best?

The lowest positions on the office totem pole take their sex where they can get it. And their pitiful couplings show no creativity at all. It's the old missionary position and that's about it. Lee and Marilyn doing the dirty deed on his desk. Dave and Lisa steaming up the car windows in the parking lot. Should you knock to see if everything is OK in there?

Jerry feels he's there just to service all the secretaries in the Law Division. Fran is fooling around with her boss. Georgia and Ted hang out at the Xerox exchanging pictures of their

Chapter 6 - Things and Stuff

private parts. That's why they are all just minions – no imagination. If you want creativity, you need to look to those that are management material.

Equal opportunity for sexual experience would certainly improve worker morale. Sadly, however, there is no equality in the sex experiences of workers. I'm sorry to break the news to you – handsome, muscular men and beautiful, willowy women have much more access to it than the rest of us. This is a real discrimination problem that all corporate Human Resource departments should work toward trying to solve.

A guy in senior management, however, has access to sex even if he looks like a toad. Those beneath seniors (so to speak) often use sex to advance in the corporation. All it takes is the promise of a quick promotion, a fat pay raise, or some really good perks. Why is that file clerk driving a new company car? Why has Suzie, who never got a college degree, just been appointed Vice President of Planning?

Why has old George Welbly taken a sudden interest in Governmental Affairs? Perhaps it's that attractive lobbyist, June. They take a lot of trips to Washington these days, don't they?

Then there was your boss, Mann. He viewed office sex as a perk. He was fond of encounters in the back of the company limousine. He thought that the company jet flying at thirty thousand feet was a great place for a good bout of get-down-to-it sex. He also found that the shower in the chairman's private bathroom made for a quality experience.

Of course, Mann was eventually booted out. Did he put his hand in the wrong cookie jar? The news release said that he had left the company "to pursue other opportunities." His wife is currently pursuing ways to attach more of his company stock in the divorce decree.

Some senior managers have sublimated their sex drive, using that energy to work incredibly long hours. For example, Stan Bobble thought that power was a far better aphrodisiac than sex. Wouldn't the rest of us be much better off if he directed his energies toward some willing partner? If he were getting a little, we wouldn't have to work so hard!

What's the biggest productivity problem in corporate America today? It's the coed nature of the work place. Think about it. Why did they used to have good Catholics separated into different schools? They had one school for boys and another for girls. Back then the kids studied, didn't they? They kept their minds on business.

Why are priests kept separate from nuns? Keeps their minds on their praying, doesn't it? Why are prisons same-sex institutions? How much repenting would be done if they weren't? Why did they keep the sexes separate in the military? How much fighting would have been done if you had fraternization in the foxholes? What about sports? What if that butt you were patting in the football huddle was of the opposite sex? How many times would the play be run correctly?

Clearly, a mixing of the sexes in the work place is a big problem. So if we want to get anything done we need a same-sex work place. On second thought, with gays making up about ten percent of the population, that won't help productivity either.

Chapter 6 - Things and Stuff

Corporate Lunacy

BOSSES ARE "BEAUTIFUL"

Why deny it, bosses are the best! Where else can you get such a flourishing of human eccentricity, such crassly colorful displays of vanity and such a *frisson* of elemental fear? These guys can end your career, no doubt about it. For as long as they last, their eight hundred pound gorilla status is, by definition, present and in working order. And you might even make it there yourself someday.

CONTROL FREAKS – The Boss From Hell

"I sit on a man's back, choking him and making him carry me, and yet assure myself and others that I am very sorry for him and wish to ease his lot by all possible means – except by getting off his back."
Leo Tolstoy (1828-1910)

It's the afternoon of your first day in Playa Del Carmen. You're just beginning to unwind after that wonderful massage and your second *piña colada*. You listen to the drone of the dive boat taking snorkelers to some distant reef. A worker swings his machete at a palm frond. Whack...it disappears.

A soothing breeze rustles through the palm trees and flutters over your *Palapa*. A ferry disappears over the horizon on its way to Cozumel. Gentle waves continually lap against the shore and pelicans fly past in precisely aligned squadrons. Occasionally a horseman rides by, galloping to nowhere in particular.

Corporate Lunacy

You wonder why the German girls are topless but the Americans are not. Hmmm…need to contemplate that one. The reverie is shattered when the bellman, Ernesto, says there was an urgent call from a Mr. Mann. That's your boss, and obviously you'll have to call him back.

Your *cabana* doesn't have a phone (you were trying to get away) so you find a pay phone. You wait for ten minutes with the phone stuck to your ear while Mann's secretary goes to find him. Lord, it's hot and sweaty in that phone booth.

Finally, Mann turns up and wants to know where you've been. You're on a vacation that has been scheduled for months. Silence. Finally: "I change my vacations when important projects are happening." He lets you know without subtlety that all aspiring executives do the same.

He asks a bunch of questions that any of your people could have answered. Then he makes a disparaging comment about how they haven't helped him much, mumbles something about commitment and hangs up.

Talk about screwing up your day! That relaxing massage is totally forgotten. Every muscle is as tight as a drum. You go back to the beach. You can't concentrate enough to read the latest Clancy novel. You've got the runs, and it has nothing to do with *Turista*. You finally get yourself settled down by about noon the next day – just in time for Ernesto to bring you a package.

It's an airfreight express delivery from headquarters. Inside are a cell phone and a note instructing you to keep it with you at all times so that you can to be reached. Likewise, there are several files and contracts for you to review.

Why is Mann such a control freak? Why did he have to be your boss? Remember, when you were a kid, what little Johnny would do when the other kids wouldn't play the game his way? He'd throw a tantrum and scream, "I'm going to take my ball and go home!" That's your boss. He can make you sit, speak, stay, rollover, play dead, grovel – good boy!

Mann must know everything and approve everything. Information is power. He parcels out tidbits of information the way that a master chef uses truffles – sparingly. He thinks having control means he's better and smarter than you are. Maybe he is. After all, he doesn't have to report to himself.

Mann loves to trash your work. When you're informed that even a chimpanzee could write better than you do, you politely inquire what the nature of the problem is. It doesn't flow right, he tells you. Now isn't that helpful? What should you do? Make it flow better (try a Cuisinart)?

Mann rewrites the report that you worked on for months, giving it his own spin, getting it wrong and producing pure blather. He communicates by criticizing, name-calling, ordering, threatening, moralizing and excessively questioning. He leaves you cowering and whimpering in the corner like a dog.

He thinks they are all against him, and they are, so he surrounds himself with yes men/persons. Guess what you are?

He makes you upset, gives you a stomach ache, anxiety,

Corporate Lunacy

depression, low self-esteem, high-blood pressure, the runs, a pain-in-the-neck and basically just pisses you off. You can't endlessly suffer the insults, humiliation, frustration and other collateral damage resulting from sordid sycophant syndrome (SSS). Very soon, you are probably going to barf, retch, heave, hug the porcelain, or lose your cookies. While synonyms are fun, this doesn't sound healthy, does it?

You can take control of your life again. All you need to do is learn the Twelve Steps Toward Recovery. You must begin healing, have a spiritual awakening, generate good vibes and gain enlightenment:

Chapter 7 - Bosses are "Beautiful"

THE TWELVE STEPS TOWARD RECOVERY

1. **Admit that you are powerless.** Your life has become unmanageable.

2. **Feel your anger.** It ain't just gas from the jalapeno taco dip.

3. **Trust your inner signals.** He really does make you want to puke.

4. **Keep your sense of humor.** However, laughing uncontrollably is a sign that you've flipped.

5. **Come to grips with reality.** The guy's truly a world class jerk!

6. **Recognize the source of the problem.** It's not you, silly, it's that anal-compulsive monster you report to.

7. **Confront your tormentor.** Be direct, courteous and calm. Don't yield to the desire to make him a eunuch.

8. **Share your feelings with him.** Forget that he has no empathy or feelings of his own.

9. **Put yourself in his shoes.** Understand that because of his deep-rooted insecurities, he has a need to abuse you so that he feels better.

10. **Ask for feedback.** Inquire whether he really considers you a worthless dog. Don't be surprised at the answer.

11. **Express your anger and frustration.** This will make you feel better but will probably make him angry and frustrated.

12. **On second thought, unless you already have another job**, just say – "Pardon me sir, would you like me to fetch?"

Corporate Lunacy

THE DOWNSIZING DEMON – A Grim Reaper

"He looked at me as if I was a side dish he hadn't ordered."
Ring Lardner Jr (1885-1933)

Well, what else did you expect after three years of losses and a declining stock price? Your company has just announced a new CEO. Carl Blades will replace the nice but ineffectual George Welbly. The new guy is from the outside and is known as a ruthless cost cutter. Carl will get a salary of $1.9 million and a guaranteed bonus of $1.5 million. He was also awarded two million shares of Acme stock and options to buy another three million shares at $10 a share.

Chapter 7 - Bosses are "Beautiful"

Acme Industries Announces Carl Blades as New CEO

CLEVELAND, Dec. 15, 1996:

Acme Industries announced Carl Blades will become its new CEO, effective immediately. Blades replaces George Welbly, who resigned to pursue other interests. Blades said, "I plan to make changes that will enhance shareholder value and move us over the bridge to the 21st century." Blades was most recently at Ajax Corp., before it was sold to a German conglomerate.

The news reported a jump in Acme's stock from $5 to $15 per share. Carl's stock increased $10 million in value, to $30 million. His options are now worth another $15 million. Carl thinks, "Not a bad day's work...and I haven't even started yet."

On Wall Street, Carl's called "Mr. 20/20" because he once bragged to an analyst that he could take any company in America and close twenty percent of its factories and eliminate twenty percent of its people. Building shareholder value is his mantra. He's coming from Chicago and he is not going to move his family. He'll just take an apartment and go home on the weekends.

Three days later, on December 18, a new headline reads:

Corporate Lunacy

Acme Announces Top Management Shakeup

The stock rises immediately $2, to $17. Carl makes a cool $10 million. Five senior managers walk, and Carl brings in two of his buddies to replace them.

Blades begins his first meeting with his staff by saying, "I wouldn't be here if this company was well run. I believe twenty percent of the people have most of the ideas and do most of the work. The other eighty percent are dragging us down. They're sheep. Some of them will soon be lamb stew."

"From now on it's long nights and weekends in the office. If you don't think you can cut it, walk out that door now. I can't stand whiners." Gee, what a nice guy. You wonder if you'll be one of the survivors.

On December 22, the company makes the following announcement:

Acme Plans to Close New Jersey Factory

This is interesting, Blades is actually closing a factory he's never even seen just to show he hasn't lost his edge. The stock price rises to $20. Carl's wealth increases another $15 million. Five hundred people are canned. Merry Christmas!

On December 29, the headline says:

> ## *Acme to Terminate All*
> ## *Consultants and Reduce R&D*

The stock moves up another $1. He's actually axed the consultants, so he can't be all bad. On the other hand, he's neutering research and development, and without that, where's the future of the company? Don't get all soft and wimpy on me now.

You should know what Carl knows: "Shareholders reward the present. It doesn't matter where the company is going to be in ten years. It matters where the stock price is now." Did I hear we were laying off another thousand workers? Gosh, Happy New Year.

Carl begins the New Year with a tour of the company's factories. By early February, he's ready for his next move. He calls his staff together again and says, "Over the last three weeks I've done an exhaustive study of our options and have made some decisions. We will close the factories in Pennsylvania, New York, Ohio and Michigan and move all of our production to the Alabama facility."

Unfortunately, Jones decides to protest, "But that's eighty percent of our facilities." Carl says, "I'm impressed that you can count. Now count your days on the unemployment line and get your butt out."

Corporate Lunacy

A few days later a news release reports:

Acme Industries Announces Factory Closings

CLEVELAND, February 7, 1997:

Acme announced today a dramatic restructuring plan. Acme will close four of its five factories and reduce its workforce by 4,000 jobs. Production will be consolidated into its Tuscaloosa, Alabama, facility. The company's CEO, Carl Blades, said, "These moves should help enhance shareholder value and move us over the bridge to the 21st century."

The stock price rises to $25.

Closing the factories means that four thousand workers earning a total of $120 million in salary lose their jobs. Would this have given you pause? If so, it's clear you're not the stuff of which leaders are made.

Carl's stock just went up by $20 million, and he's not suffering from cognitive indecision at all. The three suicide notes from former employees will go into that special circular file that God invented for messages from those who can't-cut-the-mustard.

When next month rolls around, Carl announces to his depleted but still attentive staff, "I know from experience that twenty percent of the products make eighty percent of the profit. Listen up, folks, this is where we really make some money for our shareholders."

201

The news headline the next day says:

Acme Proposes Dramatic Product Line Restructuring

In the following day's trading, Acme's price increases $4 a share.

The last thing on Carl's agenda is downsizing the corporate staff and moving the company's headquarters to downtown Chicago. The April news release reports:

Acme Corporation Announces Restructuring

CLEVELAND, April 1, 1997:

Carl Blades, the new Chairman and CEO of Acme Corporation, announced Acme will undertake a career transition program for its corporate staff. "By a combination of decentralization, outsourcing, value-engineering and rightsizing, we expect to reduce the corporate staff by 230 jobs. This should help enhance shareholder value, strengthen our global effectiveness and move us over the bridge to the 21st century." There are currently 256 people on the corporate staff.

The stock rises another $5 and Carl's investment grows $25 million.

More people are unemployed – including you. As a shareholder, you're happy Carl's built some real value in your stock. Your 2,200 shares of Acme are now worth almost $75,000. However, as an employee, things suck. You've lost a job that paid $100,000 a year. In your next move to a high profile position, you'll be able to inquire: "Would you like fries with your order?"

Why are you surprised? When Carl arrived, his press clippings came with him. You remember that headline, "Blades Says Deep Cuts Sound Surgery for Sleepy Giants." Have you woken up yet?

On Buzz-Saw Blades' Slim Fast plan, Acme is going to cross the bridge to the 21st century looking trimmer than an anorexic dancer on speed. Fifty-two percent of the blue-collar workers, sixty-three percent of the white-collar workers and seventy-four percent of the middle managers aren't coming with it. Senior management is scarcer than an ethical politician.

Carl's stock and options are now worth $140 million. In a few more months, he will sell the company and move to Florida. In all probability, as the plane takes off and he smoothes out the creases in his $5,000 suit, Carl will be thinking, "I just love building companies."

So what can you do if a Carl Blades takes over your company? Well, I have three pieces of advice:

1. **Be the first to leave.** You have a better chance of finding a job if you aren't competing with four to five thousand former employees.

2. **Be the first to leave.** Why would you want the uncertainty, heartburn, ulcers and sleepless nights you would have if you stayed on?

3. **Be the first to leave.** Even if you survived, would you like yourself? You would have to become like Carl.

THE STARMAKER – Fast Track Frenzy

"There is probably an element of malice in the readiness to over-estimate people: we are laying up for ourselves the pleasure of later cutting them down to size."
Eric Hoffer (1902-83)

Your boss, Leland Oberstar, thought that you were the greatest. He believed that you had awesome potential. You possessed super credentials and boundless energy. You were unbelievably articulate and incredibly bright. And those were just a few of the good things! You were the perfect choice for Vice President of Major Stuff. Oberstar would be your mentor. He wanted to put you on a "fast track."

Oberstar didn't recognize that these were the same things he originally thought about the last guy, Stanley. They were also his initial views of Craven and Morris and Collins and Eddy and Hill and Brown.

All those guys were put on a fast track, too. They all rode that *Star Express* on a fast, exhilarating ride, and one by one their trains

Corporate Lunacy

derailed. Morris and Stanley crashed and burned; they were canned. Hill was named VP of Dead-end Duties; Collins left for a better job; Craven now works on a tuna boat; Brown is writing a book; and Eddy has dropped out of sight.

Oberstar was always looking for a young protègè through whom he might relive his career. Obviously, with his help, that lucky fellow would avoid all the nagging little missteps Oberstar himself had made in the course of his corporate ascent.

Oberstar was a narcissist, obsessed with perfection. He wanted desperately to view himself in the mirror of these bright, flawless young people's careers. He needed these young people to love, adore and venerate him. His need was so great that he habitually convinced himself that he had finally found that perfect person.

Unfortunately, he was destined to be forever disappointed. It always became apparent that those he put on the fast track were mere mortals. Once that happened, he ruthlessly eliminated the imposters and started the search anew.

Well, at first the fast track promotion seemed like something you really wanted. Vice President of Major Stuff had a neat ring to it. Your new job would look great on your resume, and the position came with a lot more money. You could buy that Beemurr or Jeep 4 x 4 that you had always lusted for. Above all, didn't Oberstar think you were just swell?

As a fast-tracker, your star would rise rapidly like all the others. However, it would soon peak and then fall to earth.

Eventually, you would leave on your own, they would can your butt, or you would be transferred to some dead-end job. If you had continued to labor in obscurity, you might have remained employed for the long term. But that wouldn't have been the real you, would it? You dynamic devil, you!

So you ignored the warning signs and took the job. The company newspaper proclaimed how important you were. Oberstar was quoted, "I have great expectations for this young man."

At first, he proudly showed you off, much as you would display your brilliantly colored new toucan. Okay, now say something clever to his management friends, something like: "I agree with Mr. Oberstar on that." By his glowing description of you, you would have thought he expected you to single-handedly save the company.

Well, that first year was awesome. Oberstar was very supportive of everything you did. Even your mistakes were viewed as teaching opportunities. You could learn so much from his sagacity. You were enthusiastic about your job, and he was basking in the wisdom of choosing you to mentor. It was really exhilarating. Hope you enjoyed the honeymoon, because quickly your life turned to dog poop.

The next year, things began to change. Someone criticized you. There was a little tarnish darkening your brilliance. At first it was really unwarranted. You negotiated a terrific deal for the company, but the guy on the other side of the transaction turned out to be Oberstar's buddy. They were personal friends who went to the symphony together.

Corporate Lunacy

Can you believe the guy complained to Oberstar about your tactics in an attempt to weaken your authority? Whether or not it was justified, it didn't matter. As far as Oberstar was concerned, it was criticism, and you were no longer perfect.

Next, you missed a deadline. You were on vacation when something went wrong in your organization. Then you had an employee with such performance problems that you had to terminate her. Oberstar fretted: "Personnel problems! Maybe you don't know how to manage your people." Maybe you weren't a superstar after all.

Worst of all, Oberstar was becoming concerned that you might be after his job. His paranoia kicked in big time. He began to plot your downfall, telling himself that it was self-preservation. He began to disparage your contributions to senior management. He took the credit for all you did well but he blamed you for any mistake, no matter how unwarranted. You were not merely a disappointment but a cancer that needed to be surgically removed.

Was Oberstar concerned about your failure? Hardly! He relished it! Lucky for him that he had discovered Walters. Oberstar thought to himself: "I'll just put Walters on the fast track. Walters is the greatest. He has awesome potential. Walters has super credentials and boundless energy. Walters is unbelievably articulate and incredibly bright. And that's just a few of the good things. In fact, Walters is just the guy to make the Vice-President of Major Stuff. He will develop quickly under my tutelage. I will be his mentor." Stanley and Craven and Collins and Eddy and Morris and Hill and Brown and now you are just history.

It's a sad thing that Oberstar had to pick you to be the object of his bizarre desire. If you could have a "do over," what have you learned from this experience? You should have learned that you really only have a few choices, and they're all bad. So just pick the best of the lot:

1. **Blend into obscurity**. Claim family issues, health issues or anything else you can think of, but turn down that promotion. Say that the challenges of the position are too great, and you cannot devote the time required. Just realize this may be the last promotion you're ever offered.

2. **Take the promotion**. Get on the fast track, but realize the descent may be even more rapid than the ascent. Put the promotion on your resume and then begin looking for a good headhunter.

3. **Continue to be Oberstar's pupil**. What's so bad about being a sycophant, anyway? Sit at the feet of the great master and forget that mind-of-your-own nonsense. It doesn't matter what he does, he's your idol and will remain so. This choice may prolong your tenure, but it won't assure it.

Corporate Lunacy

YOU AS BOSS

"We have seen the enemy and he is us!"
Pogo (a noted management consultant)

Just look at you, strutting like a peacock, The President of the Straight Staples Division. They just don't get much bigger britches at the T. Rex Corporation than you. You're now the boss, chief, capo, honcho, head-cheese, bwana, padrone, meister... "You da man!"

My lord! Don't you know what you've done? You are now the brunt of all those "boss jokes." The things you said about Oberstar, your former boss, are now being said about you. Paranoid? You should be! The back-stabbing you did to get here may be returned in kind. You are now in charge of two

Chapter 7 - Bosses are "Beautiful"

thousand people. They don't do what you want. They talk behind your back. They don't work as hard as you do. You have to manage, trust and depend on them. People are the pits...ptuiiii!

You have begun to refer to your subordinates as "the little people." You're working on a Mission Statement and a Strategic Plan. You're making "teamwork" speeches. You're talking about management paradigms. You read management books for hours, searching for wisdom. You attend countless seminars concerning every new management fad.

Your time is no longer your own; you have meetings, meetings and more meetings, plus social engagements that you don't want to attend. Everyone is trying to see you for a decision. You just want to hide in your office.

You try different management styles, but none work very well:

1. **You try to lead by example**. But why would two thousand otherwise sane people follow you? Would you follow the incompetent you that is struggling to crawl out from beneath all that bluster? Your subordinates remember everything you say. You mumbled, "Employees are our most precious asset," and someone put it on the bulletin board. Maybe you should just procrastinate. After all, if it weren't for the last minute, nothing would get done.

2. **You try the cattle prod**. You push, prod and scare the hell out of your employees. You relish those performance appraisals. Everyone falls into line and does what you want. You kick butt and take names. With two thousand employees, there is plenty of butt to choose from. It's such great fun to see your subordinates fetch. Wait a moment. Aren't you acting like that control freak, Mann? Remember how much you hated him? You'd better avoid dark alleys.

3. **Then you empower the people**. Delegate! After all, you can't do everything by yourself. Empowerment is all the rage today. Take full responsibility for your actions − except those that are someone else's fault. You now have two thousand people to blame for your own deficiencies. Let them do their thing. Work their buns off. You can go play golf. That's what Stubblefield did. Of course, old Stubble is no longer employed. He has a lot of time for golf these days.

You've navigated the corporate jungle adroitly, but you don't know what to do next. How much money do you really need? Why aren't your eighty-hour workweeks enough to get the job done? How do those other senior executives find the time to play all that golf?

When you were promoted, you thought you had outdistanced that bastard, Steve, your rival. Then they made him President

Chapter 7 - Bosses are "Beautiful"

of the Crooked Screws Division. Now he's your rival to become the next CEO of the whole T. Rex Corporation. He's more committed to derailing your career than ever before.

Remember when you asked your employees for their "honest feedback?" Why did so many have the temerity to give it? That suggestion box was really a stupid idea. Their complaints could have filled a boxcar. Now you just want to fire them all. Unfortunately, you would spend the rest of your life fighting wrongful discharge actions in court if you did. Everyone today is in a protected group: senior citizens, minorities, females, homosexuals, members of religions, political affiliates, etc.

YOU'VE GRABBED THE BRASS RING AND IT HURTS.

You've reached the top of the heap and you don't like it one bit. Your ambition overcame your genetic propensity to be lazy, and now everything has gone up: Your work hours increased. Your stress level skyrocketed. You're drinking more. You've gained weight. Your cholesterol level is elevated. Your blood pressure is dangerously high.

In short, you have become a prime candidate for stroke, heart attack, nervous disorder, anxiety attack, ulcer, depression, or chronic fatigue syndrome. Your salary has increased, but unfortunately, your expenses have risen faster. The only real positive is that your pension and the size of your golden parachute have gone up also. It will cost them a bundle if you leave.

It wasn't supposed to be like this. You've done it all, and it wasn't worth doing. Your life has become nothing but aggravation and stress. You're just a mess. And it's lonely at the top. Your only friends are those damned consultants that you hired.

Having everything come your way really meant that you were speeding south in the northbound lane. And those employees: you can't lead, control, trust or terminate them. Maybe the time has come to consider leaving the corporation. Now, there's a positive thought.

Chapter 7 - Bosses are "Beautiful"

Throwing caution to the wind, Ralph left.

Corporate Lunacy

LET ME OUT OF HERE!

Proceed to the nearest exit with caution

When you've got to go, you've got to go – and, in my opinion, you should have gone a long time ago. Here is a short discussion on filing your corporate divorce papers and what to do in the afterlife.

INVOLUNTARY SEPARATION – Discharge

"Employees are our most important resource; let's go harvest a few."
Attila the Hun (406-453 AD)

One way out of the corporation is to wait around until they make the decision for you. There are lots of names for this particular experience. You can be fired, canned, axed, dismissed, ousted, removed, kicked out, cast off, booted, discarded, downsized, or sacked – anyway, you no longer have a job!

The whole process is euphemistically called rightsizing, restructuring, outsourcing, reskilling, re-engineering, revitalizing, or job separation. Isn't that precious? How about sugarcoating things with a work-force imbalance correction, cost saving or efficiency initiatives, differentiating the essential from the extraneous, business transformation, Enterprise Resource Planning (ERP or maybe urrrp), eliminating non-value added work or redesigning human resource systems?

Are these enough to make you lose your lunch? My particular favorite is needed holistic medicine, which positions the company for bright growth prospects. Whew!

One way to lose your job is to be part of a downsizing. For example, you could have been an employee of Blue Sky Industries when Dave Lugner, the CEO, reinvented his company. Blue Sky had 1001 employees and a total payroll of $22 million (1000 employees making $20,000 each and Lugner making $2 million). This worked out to an average salary of $21,978.

This was distressing to the Blue-Sky Board because competitors were only paying an average of $20,000 per worker.

The Board told Dave Lugner that salary costs were too high. He concluded that the only way to make the board happy was to have a ten percent reduction in staff.

Eliminating one hundred workers reduced salaries by $2,000,000. Now there were nine hundred workers @ $20,000 +Lugner @ $2,000,000 =$20 million in total salaries. Shockingly, however, average salaries had actually risen to $22,198 from $21,978. Panicky, Lugner called together a committee that recommended – you guessed it – another downsizing.

Another important reason to fire employees is to pay for new perks for senior management. Perks Per Employee (PPE) is the average number of employees who must be harvested to pay for a new perk for top management. For example, to pay for a new $40,000 country club membership, the company must downsize two employees @ $20,000 each.

Let's do a simple financial analysis of a new car program for worthy executives. A new Cadillac worth $40,000 can be paid for by harvesting two employees @ $20,000 each. A new $70,000 Mercedes can be earned with a harvest of three and a half workers. That beautiful (and well-deserved) new Rolls Royce will require a harvest of seven employees. Not wanting to be greedy, the executive decides to go for the Mercedes. So three workers are outsourced, and one is put on part time without benefits. Doesn't it give you a warm feeling to know you were part of such a worthy cause, or did you just wet your pants?

Chapter 8 - Let Me Out of Here

Most staff reductions assume that costs can be lowered while service, quality and sales remain exactly where they were. Therefore, companies just add up the cost savings of eliminating services and see how much their profits will rise. Of course, this is total bullshit (speaking technically)! Antagonized employees will defeat any potential cost savings by giving belligerent, poor service to customers. The inevitable result will be higher costs and lower sales.

There are some jobs that companies can eliminate with impunity. For instance: corporate policies, telecommunications (telephones), corporate contributions, protocol, transportation, employee activities, training and education, quality management, corporate design, forms management and food

Corporate Lunacy

service. Other silly functions include: flight operations, the barbershop, university relations, engineering services, office supplies, government relations, aircraft scheduling and the assistant to the secretary of the president. Tough cookies if you're involved.

What are some sure signs that you are likely to be involuntarily separated from your position?

1. You are selected to lead the multi-disciplinary taskforce on work place implement procurement (purchasing office supplies).
2. They build a new corporate headquarters, and you can't find your office.
3. Your key card no longer opens the door at the employee entrance.
4. You are put on special assignment.
5. You are a loaned executive to a local charity.
6. You are given an assignment to redesign the corporate logo.
7. Your title changes from vice president to chauffeur.
8. You are reassigned as liaison to the Bangladesh subsidiary.

Wouldn't you rather take action on your own than have to wait for the sky to fall? Involuntary separation is the pits!

LEAVING FOR A NEW COMPANY – Deja Vu All Over Again!

"After all, tomorrow is another day."
Margaret Mitchell (1909-49)

You answer the phone and a cheery voice on the other end introduces herself as Julie Marker. She's an associate with a national headhunting firm. She says, "We would like your assistance in finding someone to fill a six-figure job at a Fortune 500 company in the Midwest."

The company is looking for someone "who possesses strong technical skills and exhibits leading-edge management methods. The ideal candidate will be able to adapt to a fast-paced dynamic environment, will evidence excellent interpersonal and communications skills and the ability to create, and implement and manage a self-initiated agenda. This person will interact with members of senior management and collaborate with all levels of the organization."

Your heart starts to race. Talk about incredible...it's you they are describing! You can get into all that interacting, collaborating, self-initiating, communicating, creating, implementing and leading-edge, fast-paced, dynamic stuff. They are tempting you with a larger salary to try it again at a different company. Wow! They'll pay that much for you? You tell Julie that you're the guy they are looking for and she offers to send you some material to review.

Corporate Lunacy

Hold on there, trigger! Before you sign up, think carefully. Is it truly an exciting promotion that is attracting you, or are you just trying to escape from your current job? Will you achieve happiness in a new company or would you just be exchanging your room in one asylum for a similar place in another?

The following quiz may help you make a rational decision. Just answer these eight simple questions:

1. **Will you be doing boring, useless things?** Your new job may involve mindless busywork just like you do now. What if there are mission statements to write which have nothing to do with the way the company really functions? What if you have to revise the Corporate Policy Manual? What if you're destined to attend an endless series of mind-numbing committee meetings? What if quality management is talked about, written about and agonized over but not practiced? What if management addresses its problems with a new organization chart, a downsizing, or in the extreme, a new office building? What will you do if the Strategic Plan is nothing but fantasy?

2. **Will appearance be more important than actual results?** You'd better ask about the norms of appearance in the new corporation. Check out if all the senior people look the same. Do they speak the same buzzwords,

like windup dolls? See if all the promotions go to the good-looking, socially astute, confident-sounding but inept types. You may find that there are plenty of incompetent brown nosers being promoted there. You might be just another one of the faceless, cookie-cutter executives: correct suit, shirt, tie, shoes and haircut.

3. **Is everyone playing political games?** See if backstabbing games are being played in the new company. What happened to the guy who had the job before you? Did his fellow workers kick his briefcase over the cliff after him? Have they already divided up his stuff? Check to see if gossip is closer to the truth than the official company communications. Being a team player may mean that you must agree with everything the boss says.

4. **Will you have to cope with bureaucratic incompetence?** Is bureaucratic double-speak the language of choice? Do people who specialize in making the simple into the complex surround you? Are the opinions of investment bankers, consultants, brokers and any other outsiders valued more than those of employees?

5. **Will you work endless, stressful hours?** Probably. Will they find you everywhere by e-mail, cell phone, pager, faxes? You might have to spend sixty to seventy

hours per week at work and have little time for your family. They may resent it if you take the vacation you're entitled to.

6. **Will there be a class system?** What if there is a hierarchy that makes the caste system of India look like a free-floating group-grope in Berkeley? Perks and incentives may be carefully structured to demonstrate whose is bigger and whose is better. Planes, cars and country club memberships will tell which executives have the most status. It may be even worse than where you are now.

7. **Will you suffer under outrageous bosses?** Ha! You already know the answer to this.

8. **Will you be expendable?** You know those feelings that your job isn't secure. You have no authority but lots of responsibility. What makes you think your new company will be any more loyal to you than the old one? If the new organization is in terminal decline, who will be the first to go?

It's a good bet that you answered yes to all eight questions. If you didn't, was there something you didn't understand? The new institution may look pretty swell at first sight. However, the words may have changed, but the melody remains the same.

NOW THIS IS REALLY PROFOUND: Changing jobs obviously isn't all it's cracked up to be! To really improve your lot you need to leave the corporate world entirely.

A NEW CAREER – Escape

"I have found some of the best reasons I ever had for remaining at the bottom simply by looking at the men at the top."
Frank More Colby (1865-1925)

Do you want to break out of the corporate rut? Then quit your job, climb the wall and escape! Do you need some good reasons to consider this drastic step? How about the obnoxious bosses, mindless busywork, ruthless behavior, mind games and lack of any semblance of job security? You could create a pretty long list without having to hurt your head thinking, couldn't you?

Fantasize about doing what you want to do. Visualize employment that gives you good vibes. Don't be concerned that it doesn't exactly pay big bucks. Let your imagination roam, fantasize, hallucinate and envisage about your true life-interests.

Are you hanging onto that crappy job because you are trying to pay for all those necessities of life? Is that 5,000 sq. ft. home in that prestigious neighborhood really essential? Are that Sport Utility Vehicle and that big Beemurr really necessary? Is it vital that you and your wife dress in Armani suits, designer dresses, Rolex watches and mink coats?

Could you get by without that health club membership, private trainer, weekly massage, manicure and hair treatment? Must you have every new electronic gadget: cell phone, laptop, videocam and home theater system? Could the kids survive without private school, tennis and karate lessons and, of course, the *Au Pair*?

What would happen if you didn't go on an annual Caribbean cruise and a ski vacation to Aspen? Would life stop without that country club membership, season tickets to the symphony and theater, and that vacation condo?

If somehow you could exist without all that stuff, you could free yourself from the slavery of your corporate job. Of course, you're mortgaged to the hilt. It's all either leased or paid for with debt, on credit cards with nineteen percent interest.

It's pretty hard to get out from under, isn't it? There is an alternative: just walk away from it all! Go live in a cabin on a lake or a shanty at the beach. Open up a fishing tackle and bait shop.

You need to take action! Get out of there! Moving to another corporation isn't the answer. You'll just wind up with all the same old crap in a new place. You can permanently check out, but doesn't death seem a bit extreme? You could wait for a downsizing, rightsizing, strategic realignment, or other involuntary separation, but that's torture, isn't it? You can serve out your time and eventually retire. But how much longer are you able to put up with the aggravation?

Is there any option that makes sense? You must have a very short attention span. I'll say it again. The only sensible thing to do is leave, proceed, push on, go, exit. Find totally different employment outside this or any other corporation. Everyone has different things that turn them on. You need to think on your own. Use those reasoning skills that you didn't use when you decided to commit yourself to corporate life.

Maybe listing a few ideas of my own would help to get you thinking. In my younger days, I wanted to play beach volleyball, surf, drink beer and watch tanned girls in small bathing suits.

These options aren't available to me today. My knees are too shot to play volleyball; the surf's never up on Lake Erie; and my wife frowns on the girl watching.

So, other than drink beer, I've come up with the following ways to better spend my life than within corporate America:

1. **Become an author and sell a book.** Let me tell you just how happy you make a person (for example, this humble author) by buying his book. Please tell your friends that if they buy this book, my little son Tiny Tim can finally have his operation.

2. **Teach college.** I've heard that those who can, do, and those who can't, teach. However, who really wants to do what you have to do in a corporation? Oh, by the way, I think that teaching is a "can do" kind of thing (just in case any college deans or presidents happen to be reading).

Corporate Lunacy

3. **Open a wine bar or a bookstore.** Might be interesting. I just hope that I don't drink up all the profits, or get so engrossed in a book that I neglect the customers.

4. **Start a dive shop on a remote Caribbean island.** Can't make much money, but who cares? I'm not sure that I would actually even rent out the equipment. That takes too much energy. However, I'd sure be willing to talk to you about what the experience will be like and tell you who will rent the diving gear you need.

5. **Paint pictures in New Mexico.** Likewise, not a big money earner, but sure better for my sanity than working in a corporation. I can keep myself active by watching the rocks change color and the cacti grow.

6. **Become a pro beach volleyball player.** There wasn't much money in playing volleyball on the beach until recently. However, in the terms of the economist, "The supply of volleyball jocks created its own demand." Likewise, there may not be a pro beer-drinking circuit yet, but I could start my own.

7. **Get my kids to support me.** Well, now I must be hallucinating! I guess I've gone over the edge on this one.

Do you get the picture? Open up your mind – visualize. Imagine a life without the hassle of the modern corporation. Sounds pretty swell, doesn't it?

RETIREMENT – You've Served Your Time.

"On an occasion of this kind it becomes more than a moral duty to speak one's mind. It becomes a pleasure."
Oscar Wilde (1854-1900)

So, you want to retire. You've served your time – thirty years in the corporate asylum. They say: "Life is a journey, not a destination." Well, the journey was the pits so you're looking forward to the destination. Aren't you glad the career train finally stopped long enough to let you off?

When all this stuff started, you had your youth, your health, your hair and a sense of humor. Now you have a bunch of psychosomatic illnesses. Just because you laugh uncontrollably doesn't mean you have a sense of humor. Remember when you welcomed each new challenge? You felt that you could make a difference. In fact, you made about as much difference as a pimple on an elephant. Sigh! OK, that's enough about futility.

THE PARTY

They'll probably want to throw a party for you. Remember when they forced Ernie Gamble (the accountant) to take early retirement? They had a big reception for him in the cafeteria. There were lots of speeches, a reception line, and they invited his wife and kids.

It was really the final indignity for Ernie. He had to be gracious one last time to a bunch of people that he loathed. Ernie told me later that it felt like "calling hours" at the mortuary. He even overheard Stubblefield say quietly to Oberstar, "He really looks good, doesn't he?" Ernie said, "How the hell good can you look when you're dead? Do I look better than I did yesterday, when I had a job?"

When Stan Bobble retired as CEO of Behemoth Industries, things were somewhat different. They didn't just give him one party, they gave him five. They flew him to Paris on the Concorde for a party with international associates at the Eiffel Tower. They had a reception for CEOs at the Met in New York. They rented the Lincoln Memorial for a gathering of all his Washington friends. They had a shindig for local dignitaries at the country club. The office gave him a party and declared the next day a holiday. The whole thing cost shareholders twenty-three cents per share, but it was buried under "restructuring expense" in the Annual Report.

THE GIFT

When inmates leave an institution after a long incarceration, they typically are given a cheap polyester suit and twenty-five bucks. If you spent your career at the lower levels of a company, that's about what you can expect, too.

If you worked in the factory for forty-eight years, your snazzy retirement gift will probably be a gold-plated Timex. Likewise, you are probably headed for a second career at the Golden Arches because you can't live on the pension they give. Ernie was retired after twenty-five years and got a real gold Seiko. I understand he has a new position in the hospitality field (greeter at WalMart).

If you leave as an executive, expect different treatment. For a Senior VP of eighteen years, it's a matching pair of gold Rolex watches. For Stan Bobble, who was Chairman for eight years, it was a Gold Mercedes, golf clubs, lifetime country club membership, endowed chair at his Alma Mater, lifetime first-class airfare, personal secretary and office for five years, wine of the month membership, position on the boards of three companies and a partridge in a pear tree.

THE PACKAGE

In order to survive your retirement, you need what is called "a package." Timing is everything. The packages become sweeter around the time of the CEO's retirement. You get this special treatment by tapping into management's guilt.

It is easier for management to have a voluntary early retirement program than to fire a bunch of people, so they will try to make it worth your while to leave. If they really want you to leave, they can damned well pay you to do it. They can pretend you are older than you really are. They can treat you like you have twenty-five years of service rather than twenty. They can

Corporate Lunacy

give you a Social Security supplement, a lump sum, etc. All this means a bigger pension. And you can go back to work somewhere else at a ridiculously low wage.

Early retirement programs also allow the company to get rid of "nay sayers" like Ernie Gamble. Think of it: he's seen it all before. He knows that the new restructuring program won't work because the same thing was tried countless other times during his career. Even though the program has a spiffy new name, it's really just the same old warmed-over meatloaf.

CONSULTING

The company can also give you a consulting contract to come back at a higher salary than you made while you were employed. Total costs increase, but outsourcing work to former employees lowers the number of people on the payroll. You can be a modern day Lazarus and arise again from the dead – as a consultant. Long-term convicts often commit new crimes so that they can be recommitted. Well, you don't have to commit a crime to get back in; you can become a consultant.

DRESSING FOR YOUR NEW LIFESTYLE

Have you ever noticed that retirees lose their sense of taste in clothes and become color-blind? It's not a genetic defect! It's just that for years they had to wear a tie and suit. Now they are lost with no boundaries or dress code to follow. They begin to wear striped pants with checked shirts and pink sport coats with yellow and green plaid pants.

Well, I won't be like that! My Hawaiian shirt looks real swell with my turquoise bolo tie. Tell me what's wrong with my Bermuda shorts, black knee socks and brown shoes? Frankly, my dear, who cares what you look like when you are sitting on the beach with your *piña colada*?

Corporate Lunacy

Chapter 8 - Let Me Out of Here

Corporate Lunacy

APPENDIX

Can you imagine two aliens getting out of a spaceship? Let's send one to a mental institution and the other to a modern corporation. Do you think that you can tell who went where just by comparing their notes?

The Asylum

- Building with controlled access
- Elaborate pre-entry requirements
- Uniformity of dress of residents
- Internees assigned to tiny rooms
- Inmates are neurotic, supervisors psychotic
- Behavioral modification to norm
- Frequent group therapy sessions
- Visitors who add no value
- Bureaucratic regulations
- Many cognitive disorders
- Residents have lost touch with reality
- Psychopathic, egocentric and antisocial behaviors
- Psychological hedonism-pursuing pleasure, avoiding pain
- Bland institutional food
- Periodic psychoanalysis of inmates
- Depression is commonplace

The Corporation

- Headquarters with lobby guard
- Interviews, physical exam
- Cookie-cutter business attire
- Identical offices and cubicles
- Workers are nervous, boss is in orbit
- Need to conform...be a team player
- Committee meetings and task forces
- Sycophant consultants
- Policy manuals, ISO 9000
- Groupthink is rampant
- Plans and mission statements consume time
- Executives lust for perks and crave the next downsizing
- They practice Theory X management, but preach empowerment
- Employee cafeteria...Yeeech!
- Annual performance reviews
- Need I say more?

Corporate Lunacy

ABOUT THE AUTHOR

R.A.McMillan (a.k.a. Doctor Bob) was born little Bobby in Santa Barbara, California. According to his two older brothers, he was a tag-along and a pest. As a youth, the bullies pantsed him and stuffed him into his gym locker. The view through the slats probably shaped his outlook on people and institutions.

He became a corporate executive because he failed at everything else. He wanted to play trumpet in a jazz band but couldn't hit the high notes. He thought he might surf or play professional volleyball but tired of living on dog food. He wanted to be a dentist but had no dexterity and wasn't keen on blood or bad breath. He also flunked out of junior college.

He spent the late sixties packing groceries. A back injury helped him avoid the draft and gave the impetus to go back to college. He went to the University of California at Berkeley (he didn't inhale) and earned a doctorate in Economics. Where else would you go for business training? He worked for three years in the economics department of a major bank and was canned (this was before the days when he could think of himself as downsized).

This qualified him to work for the government, so he became an economist at the Federal Reserve Bank of Cleveland. He worked for three years, like the other Fed economists, an exhausting two hours per day, including coffee breaks. (It's scary what these government guys could ruin, if they had any motivation.) During this time, he had a few random great thoughts.

Lured by the siren call of industry in 1974, he became the Chief Economist of a Fortune 500 company. Soon afterward, they eliminated the department. Next, he was the Corporate Planner. Shortly, the department was gonzo. He led Corporate Development; it was nuked! On to manage Corporate Analysis and Control; ditto!

Is there a pattern here? He was Director of Investor Relations, putting a good face on a constant series of restructuring. Recently, he served eleven years as Vice President and Treasurer. That's senior management, isn't it?

Having served his time in the corporate asylum, the author has recently been paroled. His Ph.D. degree, hours spent in therapy, three courses in psychology and perusal of numerous self-help books, qualify him as Doctor Bob.

You will be amazed at the solutions he can prescribe for your life. Trust him to help you avoid the errors he made in his own career. Dr. Bob says, "Most of what is taught in college business classes is irrelevant to life in the corporate asylum." He should know, with his insider's knowledge of the institution! He's been there, done that! He's currently writing, playing bad golf and listening to reggae music.

Corporate Lunacy